The Principle Circle

You matter.
Your story matters.
I hope the stories
within help you
jump & keep jumping!

with love

The Principle Circle

**THE TRUTH WILL KEEP YOU IN THE FIGHT.
THE <u>TRUTH</u> WILL SET YOU FREE.**

———

Jamie Gilbert

Contents

Dedication

This book and it's impact is dedicated to my loving wife Amy.
You bring joy and love to to the darkest recesses of my soul. All you have
to do is be present in a room and everything changes.

Don't hide behind the rock or the cleft of the mountain. Let us see your
face. Let us hear your voice. For your voice is pleasant and your face is
lovely.

The Value Of Wisdom

———

IF YOU ARE LIKE ME, when you have a question, you want an answer. When you are unsure of what direction to go, you want someone to lay out the perfect path for you. We spend massive amounts of time in books, articles, videos, courses, and education seeking these answers. No doubt, you hope to find some here.

But here's the reality: **No book has THE answers.**

The answer you need, and will find, is not what you seek. Because it's in our search for answers that we develop the characteristic of accruing wisdom. In becoming someone who passionately accrues wisdom, we must apply wisdom. For, in the application of wisdom, we are transformed. And it's this transformation we undergo in our journey that is truly the answer.

It's not the answer we were looking for, but it's the answer that allows us to be effective in the world and transformational to and for those around us.

When you read this book, you will not underline the answers. You will find wisdom and principles to be applied. Apply the wisdom, and become the answer.

What Can I Do?

———

IT WAS A DARK PERIOD for me. Probably one of the darkest in recent memory. The new year had just started and we had been to the hospital three times in four weeks. My son and I both had pneumonia. With that illness I was not able to make a few business trips to speak with teams. That meant there were no checks coming in.

On top of all of that, my highest paying client asked for a refund for two months of our relationship. I realized I started working with that person without having a signed contract. Lesson learned.

We had bills piling up. I had just finished my time with a few clients and there was no one else waiting to sign up. I had no speaking engagements lined up for the next three months, and we were literally down to $11.47 in three bank accounts.

I remember the deepest feelings of shame and frustration. There was one point where my wife Amy came in and just sat next to me as I was sitting on the floor in our spare bedroom crying. She didn't say anything. She just sat next to me and put her hand on my back. She did exactly what I needed her to do: just be present. And her presence said, "I'm with you."

I remember the tears flowing in the moment as I hung my head. I wasn't contemplating taking my own life, but I remember finally understanding how someone could have those thoughts. My mind was flooded with thoughts of what family members, friends, and those I mentor would think if they *really* knew the position we were in. If they really saw me sitting on the floor of an empty apartment room crying.

Jamie, you're a fake, a fraud, and a phony. And it's only a matter of time before everyone finds out.

I don't know about you, but that's what shame sounds like most of the time in my life. And buying into those thoughts, is like buying a ticket to prison.

Wisdom From The Past

I remember having a conversation with my mentor Tony six years earlier about challenging circumstances. Specifically we spoke about different denominations of Christian churches and how we all get to core beliefs that bond us together.

He said, "Jamie, what I've done is I've decided on some key core truths about who God is, who I am, who others are, and how we are to walk as believers. I see these key truths as stakes that are in the ground." He motioned as though he was creating a circle around himself. "I try to live within those truths and when things get shaky, I can grab onto them."

That concept rushed back into my mind during this period. I thought about the stakes and the cricle that they made around me. The circle felt comforting when I thought about it. It felt secure. Not like the circle assured me that everything was going to be okay; but like I had a secure place on which to put my foot and propel forward.

That's when the image of the boxing ring came to mind. It felt like I was in a fight. But as I thought about the ropes, I was reminded of the stakes that Tony had mentioned. I could almost feel them catching me. I could sense their strength grabbing my back and propelling me forward. And I felt like I had a chance to keep moving forward.

But I started to wonder, what are my key core principles? What are some timeless bits of wisdom that if adhered to will continue to take me, my family, and those I influence in a beneficial direction?

A New Kind Of Fight

———

IMAGINE BEING A BOXER FROM a young age. You've put in thousands of hours in your craft. You've learned through victory. You've grown through defeat. And you are now ready for the biggest fight of your life on the grandest stage in the world. 10,000 people are crammed into a sold-out arena to watch you. Millions are tuned in, streaming the fight. You've been training for this moment for months and now it's time.

You step into the ring the way you've done many times throughout your career. Familiar music. Familiar warm-up, and a precise plan for how to defeat your opponent. Everything is just as you expected.

Just before the bell rings for the first round, you hear an unfamiliar crash. Your attention quickly broadens from glaring at your opponent to scanning the room trying to understand what just happened.

The crash was the sound of the ropes and buckles falling to the ground. It's not a sound you've heard before, because it's a place you've never been. This is now a different fight. It's unfamiliar territory.

The officials tell you and the other fighter that the rules have changed. They will still score each round and a knockout is still a knockout, but if you fall out of the ring, the fight is over.

Before you can process the change in rules the bell rings and your opponent bull rushes you.

What do you do?

I'm not asking about a theoretical what *should* you do or what you think you *could* do on your best day. If I'm honest I think I'm Jason Bourne and would take the guy out in one punch. But we all know that's not the truth. I'm asking what would *you* - who you are right now with your level of training and investment in your growth - do in that circumstance? Not from a boxing standpoint, but from a mental standpoint.

I know what I would *like* to be able to do and you probably do, too. But the answer for all of us is that we won't rise to the occasion. We will sink to the level of our training and our deepest heart's beliefs.

Most of us will never be in a boxing ring, and, honestly, we probably shouldn't seek that out. But every day we are stepping into a ring. Sometimes, the ropes are up, but most of the time the fight is evolving. The rules are changing. Our circumstances are rapidly in flux. Rarely do we feel like our situation is optimal, and often we think that if the circumstances were different we would thrive.

You can try changing your circumstances, but rarely does that change anything. It's usually that the one thing that we think will change everything actually succeeds at changing very little. We don't need a change in circumstances, we need to retrain how we think and who we are becoming. We need to enhance and sharpen our default mode of operation because as we change, the circumstances around us change too.

For some of us, we are in envirmonments where our circumstances change rapidly and consistetly. Others of us are in environments where the context changes very little. We've woken up in the same bed, gone to the same office, trained people in the same sport, or have been homeschooling in the same house for years. Sometimes it's the familiar situations that can pose the greatest danger to our personal and collective greatness.

But the truth of the matter is that circumstances cannot cause us to do anything. We choose what we do. But what we choose comes down to how and what we have trained.

Back In The Fight

THAT NIGHT IN THE BEDROOM was rock bottom. I tried reminding myself of the good things I have in life: my wife Amy, my son JJ, my family, my best friend Joshua, legs, lungs, and eyes. But even that bit of gratefulness didn't move me. I remember seeing a tweet from someone that said, "Out of the darkest of days come some of life's greatest moments." Though I know that to be truthful, it didn't change how I felt. Nothing did, really. But as I began to think about principles as the ropes in a ring, I began to see a challenge. I started to get creative and got active. And this principle came back to mind: "What *can* I do?"

I remember hearing this principle from Tony Robbins on a youtube clip some time back when he talked about the power of CANI. *What can I do* was the prompt he encouraged people to circle back to. And so I did.

I pulled out a big sheet of paper on a flip chart and wrote "Can Do List" at the top. I began listing everything I *could do* in the moment.

- Pray
- Read a book

- Read Scripture
- Send out tweets
- Send out books to people in coaching
- Create some audio tracks from our articles
- Write an article
- Create a video or a whole course
- Call coaches who I have been working with to follow up
- Send emails with videos to people coaching Division 1 women's soccer
- Be still and silent

I knew I wouldn't do all of those things, and I knew that most of those things would not produce an immediate change in circumstances. But it's amazing to see how many options one has when they are written on paper. From there, I just started on the ones I thought were most important. Simply put, I was active.

When I do this exercise with people I work with, they usually stop at two or three obvious options. But that's just the issue. When we only look at the limited options that are practical, reasonable, or likely to succeed, we are hamstrung. We are usually paralyzed because we don't think those options will do anything. Often our best ideas, and the actions that really move the needle, come from the craziest ideas that we have.

A mentor from afar named James Altucher rings in my mind almost daily: *Create the worst list of ideas possible.*[1] He has created massive wealth and impact by just trying to come up with ideas that can make companies and people excel. Everyday he creates a list of ten ideas. He calls it *exercising the idea muscle*. When he struggles, he challenges himself to create a list of the ten worst ideas possible. It's usually the worst ideas that create the best solutions. But if James is inactive waiting for brilliant ideas, like many of us do, then he will never do anything of value.

Try it yourself. If you feel stuck, write out an exhaustive list of what you can do right now. I didn't include this in my flip chart that night, but I could have done the following:

- Taken a shower
- Walked around Downtown
- Told my wife all the reasons I love her
- Gone to workout
- Cleaned the house
- Gone for a drive
- Called a friend to pray with them
- Spoken with a mentor and asked questions

And the list could go on and on. There are always options. Sometimes being active manifests itself in hustling around moving at a furious pace in getting things done. Like when I was with the Colorado Rapids and not playing - I went over and created my own workouts on the sideline. Or in sales when you just start hammering the phone and try to provide value to people and ask good questions.

Other times, we need to do things that are *patiently active*. They might be things like silence, prayer, or reading. They may not seem to directly impact your situation, but they are keeping you moving. It's like a good running back who keeps his feet moving and eyes up field while he waits for the hole to appear in front of him. If he just barrels through all the time, he will never be able to fully open his legs and scratch his potential. He *must* be active. But he needs to be patient in his activity.

The important thing is that you do not stop when you feel like your list doesn't have any *knock-out punches* on it. Let yourself go and list out the ridiculous ideas in your mind. Some will be great. Some will be laughable. Others will not be ethical and you should probably never *ever* mention them to other people! But in there, somewhere, is something that you *can* steward.

So I got to work on my list. I started tweeting out a video of me speaking to and FCA group in Colorado. I remember getting a tweet back from Ramapo College Softball, who commented on my video: "That was amazing! We have to get you out here!"

Yes!!! I called the coach immediately, sent an email and responded with some tweets. That little spark kept me moving.

I signed books and wrote hand-written letters to high school athletic directors across Colorado. I recorded some audio tracks, and really applied myself to providing value on Twitter.

Nine days passed and nothing transpired; at least, nothing that I could see. The softball team didn't respond to anything. The books hadn't even reached the desks of the athletic directors, and there was no response from the sixty emails I had sent.

I knew it at the time, but it wasn't what I wanted to hear: The most important part of this whole thing was who I was becoming by being active in that situation. It wasn't about booking an event. It wasn't about making money. It was about who I was becoming. And that period of time radically transformed my character.

As it turns out, I started working with a full-time client on day ten who got my book from his friend who drives for Uber. If I hadn't been active, there is no way I would have given his friend a book. From there, I have developed many relationships that stemmed from that period of activity. Joshua even played golf with one of the athletic directors who received a book. He was blown away. He still hasn't reached out to me. YET!

I've learned that often times, it's not the immediate change in circumstances that we need most. We need to see our trying circumstances as contexts for deepening and developing our character. And it's the principles in life that can help us do just that.

The Truth About Mental Toughness

———

I HEAR A LOT OF people in leadership roles and on television talk about being mentally tough. But when I ask people what they mean by that, the definition is usually muddled, at best. They can't give a definitive answer. So how can you expect those you lead to live mentally tough if you can't define what it is? Moreover, how can you expect them to be mentally tough if you're not modeling it?

A common thread in people's understanding of mental toughness is the trait of refusing to give up. Marcus Luttrell's account in *Lone Survivor* is a good depiction of how most think of mental toughness. After falling down a few hundred yards of boulders and jagged rocks, and after a vicious gun fight, he finally made it to the bottom of the mountain with a broken back, fractured femur, shattered face, and a whole host of gruesome injuries.

He knew he had to keep moving so he grabbed a rock and drew a line in front of himself in the dirt. He dragged his body until his toes went past the line. Then he drew another, and did the same. As I heard him share the story I thought he did this for a hundred yards. He did this for a few miles!

As jaw-dropping as that is, refusing to give up is only a *piece* of mental toughness, not its entirety.

My best friend Joshua Medcalf developed an awesome definition of True Mental Toughness:

> Having a great attitude
> Giving your very, *very* best
> Treating people really, *really* well
> Having unconditional gratitude,
> Regardless of your circumstances

I love that definition and support it wholeheartedly. What he is really getting at is that true mental toughness is living according to *principles,* regardless of what is happening around you and regardless of how you feel.

Mental toughness is not about suppressing emotion and sweeping it under the rug. It's not about always being even keel. It's not the ability to feel no pain and become a machine who never misses. It's deeper than that.

Real mental toughness is the ability to acknowledge your feelings, acknowledge your doubts, and acknowledge your circumstances, without letting them deter you from doing what is most important and most beneficial. It's the ability to live according to principles, regardless of your circumstances.

Let's face it, we all have days and moments where we don't feel like doing what is most beneficial. But some of us act despite how we feel and others of us don't. The great Julius Erving once said,

"Being a professional is doing the things you love to do on the days you don't feel like doing them."

But how many of us do that? If you had to place a percentage on how much of the time you live according to feelings or circumstances, what would that percentage be?

In order for us to live according to principles we have to start identifying what our guiding principles are in life.

You may not know them off the top of your head and you may only have a few. But we need to make a start, now.

Principles: The Ropes That Keep Us In The Fight

———

IN THIS BOOK I HAVE selected core principles that have radically altered my life. Like the principle from the last chapter "What can I do?" This strategy, mantra, or truth continues to propel me forward when I meet resistance and challenging situations.

I've also chosen principles that consistently help people that I get to work with. These are people in professional sports, to moms that raise their children at home; from presidents of large companies, to men and women who are coaching in high school; from people who mentor thousands of professionals, to nine year old Ty who I get to train in soccer. These principles are timeless, span the breadth of experiences, and are relatively simple.

The Principle Circle has become a regular exercise for me and people I get to work with, and I hope it becomes a valuable tool for you too.

First off, what is a principle?

It's a moral rule, belief, theory, truth, or law that influences your actions or explains how something works. They are guidelines that you choose to live by that will take you and others in a benficial direction. You can find a principle by asking this question: *What are some keys to success in my context, that if I adhere to will elicit greatness in me and others around me?*

So in golf, maybe it's that your back swing needs to be slow and smooth, you need to keep your body quiet, you don't rush through your process, and make sure that you are talkative on course.

In soccer, my keys to success were to be very communicative on the field, stay in an athletic stance, contain attackers instead of committing and diving in after the ball, and look over my shoulders constantly.

Maybe as a parent you need to get on your knees and make eye contact with your toddler, you need to take time to fill your own cup, ask questions more than you give directions, and fully engage when you child is playing.

Maybe in your business it's asking good questions and then shutting up, treating people like people instead of production units, do the most important things first, and communicate clearly and concisely.

I don't know what the principles are for you in your various contexts, but I know you can find them with these two questions:

What are some keys to success in my context, that if I adhere to will elicit greatness in me and others around me?

What are ten things I know now that I wish I knew five years ago?

Go ahead, write out ten things.

The Principle Circle In Action

———

BEFORE WORKOUTS OR AT THE beginning of my day I will create a circle of eight to 16 lines. I will write out a principle for each line that I choose to live by during the workout or for the rest of the day. Sometimes they are the same. Other times I change some according to the context I'm entering. Sometimes I do a mini one of four principles audibly as I walk into my daughter's room to bounce her back to sleep.

(<u>Full disclosure</u>: I don't do this *every day* and I don't do it before *every* event. I do it consistently, but not constantly. But in the beginning, I did it just about every day.)

I don't really care about the number. The important thing is that we are priming our minds to operate in the most beneficial manner, knowing that our practice, workout, meeting, call, class, and day will likely throw countless obstacles at us.

I remember playing golf with a young girl a few years ago. She played at a high level but did not putt particularly well on the day. On the drive between hole six and seven I asked a simple question: *What are some of your keys to success in putting?*

She said that keeping her head still through impact with the ball was the most important one.

I never said another word about it. But for the next three holes, her head stayed extremely still and she rolled the ball straight in the cup.

There was no magic involved. She simply primed her mind to focus on a process component, head still through impact, that elicits her best work. She could have missed all three putts and I still would have smiled because priming your mind to execute on principles doesn't guarantee a result. It just increases your likelihood to commit to controllables and gets you focused on growth rather than score. And that's where our greatness comes out.

The principles cut out the mindlessness that we can carry into familiar, yet very important situations, and they can help quiet the doubt and anxiety that we face when entering challenging scenarios. The principles don't change our circumstances, but they can change how we see and operate within our circumstances.

Here's what a principle circle could look like in a few different situations.

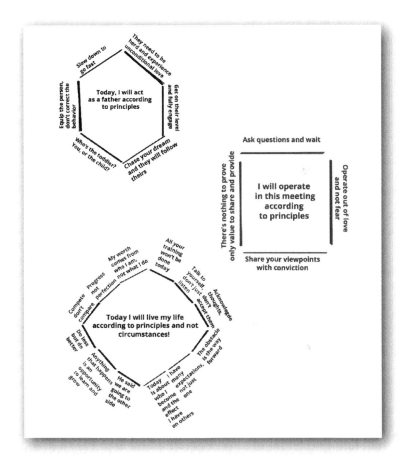

I know that these are not exactly circles, and I really don't care what shape you make them. I care about what it is and does, over and above how it looks.

Right now I'd encourage you to make your own circle of four to eight principles. Go for it.

If you want to expand it further, fantastic. But you don't have to. It's not about how many you have, it's about whether or not you choose to live by them.

WRITE IT DOWN

Throughout this book, and as consistently as you want, I'd encourage you to create your own principle circle. Like actually write it out with pen and paper. If you want the how-to guide on writing it out, or if you want to see how others create their's, visit www.t2bc.com/pcircle

And I would love to see your circle, so please share it with me!

Twitter: @Jdgilbert19
Instagram: @Jdgilbert19
#pcircle

In this book, you will find principles you can apply. The principles can be chapter headings, subtitles, quotes, verses, or your own interpretations of a concept that stands out to you in each chapter. I'd encourage you, as you read this and any other book, to write out the principles that connect with your soul. Many of us are reading and engaging with lots of content, but too many people are wearing the amount of books they have read as a badge of honor. I doesn't matter how much you have read if what you have read hasn't been applied and hasn't changed you. We don't really need to know more; we need to do more with what we know. (This could be a principle for you)

Again, I don't care about how many principles you have, I care about you choosing to live by them, and in the beginning, the best way to do that is to write them out. As time progresses you will likely notice that you do some of them subconsciously. Others, you will have greater difficulty with. But always know you have the tool of writing out those principles.

Hear me clearly, though: writing it down doesn't mean anything in particular is going to happen.

James Hahn really wound me up last year. He won a PGA Tour event at Riviera the week after Pebble Beach. After he won, the cameras zoomed to a picture of what he wrote on his glove: "Be Great!"

I'm not really upset at James. In fact, he is one of my favorite guys to watch! I'm upset with what people did with that snapshot. Sure enough there was a young kid in college that came up to me and showed me his glove right before he was about to play. It said "Be great," and he just smiled.

I don't know what he shot that day, but I know he didn't win the tournament, and I'm certain that his score wasn't pretty. There's nothing magical about writing things down. The *"magic"* happens when you *apply* the principles that you write down consistently regardless how you feel. There are no fixes. There's no pixie dust. There is training, plain and simple.

But when we write things down, we are priming our minds to find the opportunities to lean into chaos and difficulties and live according to choice, not context. Like the ropes on the boxing ring, these principles are timeless morsels, that if lived by, will help us not only survive, but throw us back in the ring and thrive.

- Do you already have principles that are coming to mind?
- What principles would you encourage your younger self to understand and live according to?
- How many principles do you want to commit to writing out consistently during the next week?

Anything That Happens Today Is In My Best Interest And An Opportunity To Learn And Grow

––––

"JAMIE, JUMP ON THE PHONE with this lady. She wants to do a workshop with us but I am working with another team when she wants to do it. The money is on the table and everything is set up. Just call her and it should be pretty easy."

I was pumped to receive that call from Joshua. I was just coming off of one of the hardest two-month periods financially and health-wise in my life. Not only did I want to speak and engage, my family needed the money.

What's interesting in life, is that we usually sink not only to the level of our training, but the level of our deepest heart beliefs. One of my deepest heart beliefs at the time was that I was terrible at getting on the phone with strangers, especially women.

My belief dates back to when I was in middle school. I used to get on our cordless house phone to call up a cute girl. I don't really know why I tried to keep calling girls because I hated it. And the worst thing in the world was the dreaded seven seconds of silence: that pause where you both know that you have nothing to say to each other that really matters. That was the most awk-wardly painful experience in life at the time. I'm sure you know what I'm talking about.

So I developed a plan to make the calls a little less stressful. Before getting on the phone I would take out a yellow legal-pad of paper and write a list of things we could talk about. And then, I created the first drop-down menu. I decided that if she talked about a certain topic, I wanted to have other topics that somewhat fit the conversation. I made a flowchart of topics that I could segue into if I felt that weird silence coming. That list of viable solutions was my security blanket. I know, real Casanova stuff!

Through repeated miserable phone calls I developed the belief that I am inherently horrible at talking to women on the phone. If I was a *natural*, this would all come easy to me like it did for a childhood friend Brandon.

Fast-forward eighteen years, and here I am about to call a lady in coaching. Nothing in that belief had changed because I accepted it as true, and never practiced getting on the phone and learning how to converse. So I did my usual practice of writing everything down on the note pad. I dialed the number and she didn't answer.

Then something came up that I hadn't planned for: the voicemail.

So I started in on leaving a message. But midway through I said something that just sounded a little goofy and I paused...for about seven seconds!

1 Mississippi
2 Mississippi
3 Mississippi
4 Mississippi
5 Mississippi
6 Mississippi
7 Mississippi

I was screaming inside!!!

I thought about hanging up, but I knew she could hear me. I've had a deviated septum since childhood and my breathing is always heard on the other end of the phone!

How do you recover from that? It was uncharted territory for me. It was my *exact* worst nightmare!

We speak all over the country about the importance of the growth mindset. We teach people to believe that anything that happens today is in our best interest and an opportunity to learn and grow. That is a brilliant principle, but sometimes it's not what we want to hear in the moment!

This thought yelled in my mind: *Alright mental training ninja! Everything is in your best interest, right?* That thought was more shame than it was encouragement. But it kicked me into gear nonetheless. So, I thought about all the options I had.

First thought, "I know there's a button on this keypad that will allow me to erase and re-record the message. I just don't know which one it is!"

So I went through the entire keypad: 1, 2, 3, all the way to zero. And nothing happened. By this time I was sixty seconds into this awful message and the only thing I accomplished was playing a musical melody on her voicemail.

Then I figured that the message might time out and there would be a prompt asking me if I wanted to re-record.

Just to cover my bases, I pulled out my computer and googled how to erase a voicemail. The first site that popped up said "99% of voicemail services will allow you to erase and re-record if you press the # key."

Lovely! Maybe I forgot to press that one.

    # - Nothing happened.
    # - Nothing happened.
    # - Nothing happened.

And then the prompt did come up and just said, "Goodbye."

It was one of those slow movements taking the phone from your ear and gently laying it on the table while trying to bottle up the emotions inside of you! I took a deep breath, eyes closed, and felt like shouting out some deep obscenities (I'm not encouraging people to curse, but if we're honest sometimes those words are the only ones adequate enough to describe our pain).

I simply recited the principle, *Anything that happens is in my best interest and an opportunity to learn and grow.*

This is not putting a positive spin on things. This is the heart of the growth mindest. It simply reminds me of the truth that the greatest teachers in my life have been difficult circumstances and failures that I have chosen to learn from. Though it doesn't feel great, I have the opportunity to learn from everything and be sharpened for the next day.

This time saying the principle wasn't shame. That was mental training at its finest. Reciting that principle didn't change the circumstances. It didn't really even change how I felt. But it did change my point of focus. It allowed me to use the emotions I was experiencing and find the most beneficial way to move forward.

It allowed me to ask the growth mindset question: If I could do this situation over again, how would I do it differently?[2]

Immediately I knew I could have embraced the silence and said, "Sorry about that, I'm not sure what just happened there, I got a little scared." I know that authentic vulnerability is the one thing that truly connects people, and I missed a massive opportunity to be vulnerable.

I also decided that I would no longer get on the phone trying to prove myself and avoid awkwardness. Rather, I would ask questions, share stories where they fit in, and be willing to get weird with people. It's amazing what can happen when instead of trying to prove ourselves, we simply try to provide value.

So I jumped back on the phone and left another message apologizing for the awkwardness and asked her to call me back.

I still haven't heard from that lady to this day!

Regardless, that call was one of the best things that has happened for and to me over the last five years. It wasn't exactly rock bottom, but it felt like it. It felt like the worst-case scenario. And since that call, I have had very little fear jumping on the phone with people. Every time I get on a difficult call, I know that it cannot be as bad as *that* moment. And now I know simple principles that I will stick to on the phone.

Prepared By Choice
A few months later I was getting ready for a call with a company that wanted to bring me out to speak. During my flight to another event I reflected on that terrible phone call and one other that I absolutely bombed out of fear. I asked the question: *"How would I do those differently?"*

I wrote out how I'd have approached them and what number I would require for my services on this call. Lastly, I wrote out two questions that I was interested in hearing responses to. Though I was writing, this wasn't a script that I was trying to not screw up. They were prompts of important information that I wanted to share and elicit from the company.

When I got on the phone, I asked a question, listened, and shared a story. Then the vice president of the company said, "Let's do a half-day keynote."

Super! But my curiosity took me deeper, and I asked another question. "How do you all praise innovation in your company?"

He said, "Actually we're not great at it. Can you share some on that?"

I did, and they doubled both my time and what they were going to pay me.

The only reason I had the ability to ask that question was from experiencing my worst-case scenario and then *choosing* to learn from it. And that's the epitomy of the growth mindset. Carol Dweck's research for over twenty years has shown that we all fall into a fixed mindset or a growth mindset.[3]

In the fixed, we see ourselves as being born inherntly incapapble of excelling in particular areas. Like me, we can say "Brandon was born able to talk to girls. I suck at it." And if that's your belief, you don't put much effort into changing it. When we believe that our traits and abilites are etched in stone, or *fixed,* we cannot see the opportunities to grow and live a different story.

However, when we adopt that growth mindset of believing that we can grow in every area of our lives, we begin to seek out opportunities where most simply see failure. But it's quite simple: in the fixed mindset, you cannot use mistakes to grow.

We've all heard the addage that our mistakes are our best teachers. I'm not sure who said it, but whoever repeats it is just as wrong. Mistakes are not our best teachers. Mistakes will absolutely eat us up, unless we consistently *choose to use* our mistakes to learn and grow. The only way we can do that is if we approach each moment as an opportunity to be refined, not as a performance we can't screw up! When it's about growth, our self-worth is off the table.

I wonder what some of your deep-seated beliefs are about yourself? Think about the worst-case scenario that embracing those beliefs might bring about. I'm willing to bet that if you place yourself in that situation, you will find that it's not as bad as you think it will be. It may hurt. It will most likely be embarrassing. But if you choose to believe that anything that happens is in your best interest, you can use that experience as a springboard to a new level of execution.

The question you need to ask is, "What am I missing out on because I am not willing to embrace my fear?" What are other people you lead missing out on because of your unwillingness to get uncomfortable? That blown call lost me the opportunity to make a good chunk of money in a weekend. But the residual benefit has allowed me to not only make exponentially more money, but it has allowed me to have a far greater impact with far more people ever since.

When you believe that anything that happens is in your best interest, you become an unstoppable force. But that belief is a constant choice. It's a guiding principle that, if lived by, will radically alter how you live, interact, create, and execute. But it's your choice, and your choice creates your challenge.

- When in the past have you successfully used a mistake or setback to make you better?
- What mistake or setback are you beating yourself up for or dwelling on right now? If you could do it over again, how would you do it differently?
- What contexts are you getting ready to enter that you are nervous about or have consistently bombed in the past? What are some key principles that you can focus on now in preparation?

What Was Does Not Determine What Will Be

———

WE DON'T HAVE TO DO what we have always done; we don't have to experience what we have always experienced. We can create a new normal when we begin living according to principles instead of circumstances. But it's a challenge. It doesn't happen by flipping a switch. It comes through awareness and intentionality.

For a few months, Amy and I played on a co-ed indoor soccer team with some friends. All of the ladies on the team played at the NCAA Division 1 level, and most of the husbands did, as well. Amy and I only lasted a few months with the team, partly due to Amy's sixth concussion, but also due to limitations on our time and frustration.

The time part of it was due to being with my son, JJ. The frustration stemmed from many of our games ending in some sort of fight. Inevitably, one of the husbands would have to get an opposing player in a headlock because he was fighting with one of our wives. Like real fights with fists and kicks.

Don't blame the guy on the other team. It was usually one of our wives that started the fight!

These ladies are lovely and I love them to death off the field, but when they lace up their boots, it's like they slip back into how they operated when they played at a top-level eight years ago. Their behavior and choices on the field are radically different than what they are off the field. The triggers of getting on the field and lacing up the boots do not change *who* they are. Rather, the triggers change the principles by which they operate. We all face that difficulty.

I remember hearing Michael Franzese[1] tell his story of being the most feared mob boss in America and then choosing to follow Christ and leave the mob. Though he has undergone a radical transformation, when he goes back to New York and is treated poorly by someone, he openly admits getting that urge to *do something about it.* I can only imagine what kind of things fall into that category!

Our circumstances have an alluring effect on how we choose to behave. But it's just that, an *effect.* It's not a requirement for Michael to want to strangle the lady who was rude to him at Starbucks, and it's not a foregone conclusion that my friend has to two-foot the guy in our recreational indoor league. That said, our environment and the stimuli within can trigger long-trained impulses that cause us to do what is usually less than beneficial.

Think about when *you* get around a certain group of friends from college or childhood. How do you start to act around them? What kind of things change in your language? What kind of actions do you begin to engage in? What changes in your perspective on life?

Sure, you can spend less time with them, and in many cases you probably should. But regardless of the environment, you need to ask yourself how you are training to be different. Remember, when you point the finger at your circumstances, there are always three fingers pointing back at you.

If you haven't trained the ability to use your emotions, then your emotions will consistently use you. If you are not actively trying to be solutions-focused in your life, you will probably remain problem-focused in difficult situations.

Many of us will say that we want to change. But I don't care about what you want. I care about what you are willing to do to close the gap between who you are and who you want to become. Because as you close that gap, you will do some really cool stuff - greater stuff than you could have ever dreamed!

I'm not going to tell you the right or wrong way to do things. I don't believe there is a right or wrong way to approach life. I believe we all have strategies that we are employing that have us where and who we are in life. My question is how is your strategy working out for you? I care that you are adopting the most beneficial strategy for you, your family, those you influence, and the world at large.

I believe in strategies, but I also believe in truth. I believe that God created this world and he is alive and active. I believe He is the only source from which one can derive real security and everlasting joy. I believe that following Jesus is the only way to truly know Him. I believe he is waiting with arms wide open for each of us to not only embrace him, but continually lean on him. And these truths are the epicenter of what I write and how I try to live.

I'm not saying that you have to believe what I believe, but this is what I believe, and I want that to be clear.

Regardless of what you believe, I care about you. Not what you've done, not what you're doing, or what you could ever do in the future. I care about you, as a person.

It breaks my heart to engage with people who are stuck in life - not just stuck in a career or a rut, but who feel lost, helpless, and feel like the only ones in the struggle. It breaks my heart because they are not the only ones. I may not be in your exact situation, but I struggle immensely, and as I work with people at the highest levels of sport and business, I know we are *all* struggling. And there is community in the struggle.

You're not alone, and I hope that in this book you will learn to unclench your fist of anger and despair, open your hand, grab on and join me and countless others who are uncomfortably embracing the courage to move forward, train, pivot, and thrive.

No one has it all together. No one is perfect in their behavior, and no one is immune to the struggle. So don't hide it. Don't fight it. Embrace it for what it is, and let's move forward together closing those gaps. Because history does not repeat itself; people repeat history when they assume that what *was* determines what *will be*.

Acknowledge Don't Accept

———

So, THERE I WAS IN October, standing in a gym about to do my first CrossFit workout. It was the beginning of my twelve-month pursuit of getting into professional level training.

I looked to my right and there was a woman getting her weights prepared. The first thing I noticed was that she was wearing the real CrossFitter apparel. She looked legit.

The second thing I noticed was the definition in her tricepts. I thought it might just be the lighting, but as she moved, so did the chisel on the back of her arm.

The third thing I noticed was that she had more weight on the bar than I did.

Then, lastly, as she turned to the side, I noticed was that she was pregnant. Not pregnant, like a little bump just starting to show. She was five months pregnant!

All sorts of thoughts started floating through my head:

Jamie, you don't belong here.
Jamie, you are going to look stupid.
Jamie, go grab some more weights.
Jamie, she has more muscle than you do.
Jamie, you can't make it in professional soccer. Look at you!

Sound familiar? Your thoughts might be a little different in content, but if you are similar to the countless people I work with and know, then there is likely little difference in direction.

Did you know that we have between 30,000 and 70,000 thoughts that go through our heads in a day?

According to studies, the majority of those thoughts are negative. And according to experience, most of those thoughts are limiting, destructive, and simply untrue.

The scarier part is that between 80-90% of those thoughts are the same thoughts we thought yesterday. Therefore, 80-90% of the thoughts we have tomorrow will be similar in form and content to what we think today.

If you don't believe me, or even if you do, I'd encourage you to take a notebook and track some thoughts. Every hour on the hour today, take three minutes and jot down the thoughts that you can remember entertaining and running with. Categorize them however you want to, but notice the trends.

We don't need to spend time trying to *correct* our thinking. We need to work on observing our thoughts.

Here is a common misconception: thoughts are not our self-talk. I remember my business partner Joshua sharing that in my house in Denver and it stopped me dead in my tracks. I had always believed that thoughts were the same as self-talk. For far too long I had beat myself up because I couldn't control what people said I should be able to control.

Thoughts are ideas or words or pictures that float through our minds that we cannot control. Self-talk is what we *intentionally* say to ourselves. You cannot control whether the thought of not being good enough comes into your mind when you see someone excelling in his or her field. That thought comes in without permission.

You cannot control thoughts, but you can choose whether or not they control you. For too long, most of us have been under the control of our thoughts because we give them power. But in reality, thoughts are more suggestions of explanations to the circumstances around us.

Yes, the pregnant lady did kick my tail in that workout. Much of it had to do with the fact that she has consistently trained for three years and I was only just returning to a heart rate above 120 beats per minute. However, some of it had to do with the thoughts that I chose to accept instead of acknowledge.

ACCEPTING THOUGHTS

Imagine you have your iPhone out. If you click on the home button twice, you can pull up all the apps that you have open on your phone. Many of us will have between fifteen and thirty apps open. With the swipe of a finger, we can flip through the apps watching them slide past us effortlessly.

I want you to think of each one of your apps as individual thoughts that are floating through your head. We have the power to acknowledge or observe thoughts and continue flipping past them. But most of us have grown accustomed to clicking on the first one.

Have you ever clicked on an app when you didn't mean to? You were intending to go to your calendar to see if you can make the date that someone requested through email. But you accidentally clicked on Twitter. As soon as it opens, Twitter has not only consumed the entirety of your screen, but it's become the entire focus of your attention.

While you were thinking about responding to Jim's request for lunch, you end up seeing a picture of one of your peers who has been crushing it in the professional league. You start thinking about how lucky she is and how great she must be to play at that level, and then you question yourself. *Look at you, you're not do anything with your life!*

That, or you click on the first business article that pops up on your feed that unpacks the exponential growth of a start-up created by a fifteen year-old. Then your mind floats to how lazy and ill-equipped you are to create something like that. You think about how *lucky* some people are. Then you think about the *unlucky* experience you had recently in not getting the job you applied for. Then you draw to mind all of the projects that you haven't finished. Then you feel anxiety because you don't feel like you will ever make six or seven-figures. Then you feel deeply unmotivated to move, let alone respond to Jim's request.

These are what people call rabbit trails, but I call them death slides. It's what we do when we allow ourselves to accept our thoughts as reality. They are not reality. They are thoughts, assumptions, best guesses, and conclusions we draw that are not based on real evidence or truth.

The reality is, you and I have trained ourselves to see those thoughts as truth, and our immediate reaction is to comply and jump on the slide.

Much of the pain in our lives is coming from the repetition of clicking on thoughts and zooming in on them, giving them power. We don't have to accept them, but we can acknowledge them.

ACKNOWLEDGING THOUGHTS

I had a girl ask me a question on the golf course one time. It was a rainy day, temperature in the forties and I had just stroked a wedge to fifteen feet. I was pumped!

She looked at me and said, "Jamie, how do you stay positive in this weather for five hours?"

Without hesitation, I said, "I don't." Her face showed the tension: *Wait, you're a mental trainer. You have to talk about being positive. That's what everyone talks about. You can't just be angry and upset. What is going on?*

I finally said, "I don't try to stay or be positive. I acknowledge the situation and I acknowledge my thought. I literally just say the thought out loud sometimes. Of course I would rather be playing in shorts and short sleeves. Of course I don't like having that one annoying drop of rain that gets in the neck of your rain suit and trickles down your back. I acknowledge it for what it is. I say, "*I don't like this.*" But I don't stay there. I focus on doing what is most beneficial."

She didn't seem to like my answer. Maybe because the *fix* wasn't quick enough, or maybe she thought I was full of crap. Many people do, and some apologize years later.

But I'm not born with a special ability. I have experience and I have practice. Part of it is the perspective that I have been training for years. I believe that anything that happens is in our best interest and an opportunity to learn and grow.

The other part of it is that I have been observing patterns of thoughts for the last two years. Not like tracking them on spreadsheets, but being aware of consistent trends in my journals and reactions to circumstances. I know when I play or train I am going to have thoughts that come up comparing myself to others or arbitrary standards. I know I am going to have thoughts telling me that I cannot make it through the workout. I know I am going to feel fatigue in particular muscles and will have thoughts trying to rationalize quitting. I know my kids will likely wake up earlier than I hope in the morning and I will think about how lucky others are who don't have kids. But those things are not what I have to zoom in on.

Just having those thoughts does not make you a lesser human being. The presence of those thoughts means nothing about you!

Those crazy ridiculous thoughts float through the minds of just about every human on the planet. So, instead of getting angry when a thought comes up or acting like it's not there, say the thought out loud, laugh if appropriate, and move on to engaging in the next piece of your activity.

I don't find much benefit in sweeping those thoughts under the rug, acting like they don't exist either. It's like a friend of mine whose ex-girlfriend walked into a friend's barbeque. My buddy tried to act like he didn't see her and like he was *cool*. He spent the majority of the next hour not engaging with or enjoying the company of his friends because he was trying not to let his feelings come out. Trying to play it cool means you are usually getting played!

But another friend hit the pressure release valve. He brought the ex-girlfriend over, said "Hey, didn't you two date for a while? Weird!"

Everyone started laughing, including the guy and the girl. It was a moment that broke the tension and allowed everyone to fully interact and engage (I do not think this is the *best* strategy for every awkward situation, but it worked in their context.).

When we acknowledge what we see and how we feel about it, we often strip the thought of its power.

REALLY BIG HANDS
I remember sitting on the bus outside of Toyota Park in Chicago. We were getting ready to play an exhibition match against the

Chicago Fire reserve team. At this point in my journey, I did not have a contract with the Colorado Rapids, but they were still allowing me to train and play with the reserve team. I was hopeful that a good performance could finally secure a contract.

As the team started to get off the bus, I grabbed the strap of my bag and looked up. The guy in front of me had grabbed the headrest and my eyes locked onto his hands. He had some massive banana hands that seemed to envelope the entire seat!

I kid you not, the thought that came into my head was, *"Damn his hands are huge! To play professionally, you have to have big hands. Jamie, your hands are small. So…"*

I went down that all too familiar death slide for a few seconds focusing on how I wouldn't get the result that I wanted, feeling less and less secure as a person and certainly not focusing on controllables. But as I stood from my seat, a huge smile came to my face. Why? Because I had acknowledged the thought and the pattern I was heading down.

At this point you can choose what to do. Acknowledging the thought gives you power. You can choose to dispute the thought like a good lawyer. I could have started naming the evidence that proves that thought has no foundation. For instance, Lionel Messi has very small hands. And he's *pretty* good at soccer.

Another option is acknowledging the thought, and turning towards something more helpful, such as saying a go-to verse from scripture, sowing a beneficial belief, being active in doing something controllable, or just engaging with other people. The choice is yours about what you do next, but it's imperative that we practice acknowledging the thought before we accept it as true.

Without a doubt, one of the greatest inhibitors to your personal, and our collective greatness, is the consistent practice of accepting limiting thoughts. Notice I said "practice." The way we engage with our thoughts is a learned behavior. It works according to a pattern we've followed for a very long time. But the good news is that we can train a new way of operating.

Today, and only today, take three minutes every hour to write a few thoughts that you engaged in during the last sixty minutes. As you look at those thoughts, are they helpful, beneficial, or true?

Also, think on this:

- What contexts will you be in today where limiting thoughts are sure to fly in?
- What are those thoughts?
- How would you like to operate when those thoughts come?
- When they hit, what truth will you turn back to?

Progress Not Perfection

———

A MENTOR OF MINE USED to fly for the Navy. He asked me a great question:

"If a Boeing 747 is flying from San Francisco to Hawaii, how much of the trip do you think that the plane is perfectly on course?"

I said, "Maybe seventy percent of the time." He assured me it was much less. Maybe only like five percent. He said that the only time the plane is perfectly on course is right when it takes off and right before it lands.

We aren't aware of it, but the planes we fly on are consistently knocked off course the majority of the time in the air. Whether it's the wind, the pressure in the air, the sloshing of the fuel, or people getting up and moving around the cabin, the plane is consistently off course. However, the autopilot works in a way where it gives these gentle nudges back and forth that knock it back on path.

That's a beautiful picture of what life is like. We all feel the resistance. We all have lapses in judgment. We all make choices that we know are not in our best interest. We all feel the blows that knock us off course. But what really drives us towards our personal and collective greatness and puts us back on course is the grace of the nudge.

It's giving us the grace to fail and to squander opportunities, but learn from them without condemnation. It's really the crux of the growth mindset where we believe that anything that happens is in our best interest and an opportunity to learn and grow. But how many of us give ourselves that grace? How many of us give that grace to those we lead? How many of us give that grace to the celebrities we see on TV?

If we are honest, most of us look at the failure, the laziness, the lack of motivation, the missed shot, the blown presentation, or slip in discretion in our own lives as evidence that we are not people or teams who are going to *make it*. We have this crazy notion that people and organizations that excel don't face the same resistance we do. And we certainly don't believe they have the same lapses in performance or behavior.

DON'T DEMAND WHAT YOU CANNOT DELIVER YOURSELF

I remember a friend I got to work with, who coached college basketball. We were on the phone and he began to unpack his frustration about his inability to keep his personal commitments of reading, character scorecard, and what went well journal. I encouraged him to think about the things that got in the way of doing those exercises, think about how he could pivot, and get back at it the next week.

A little later in the conversation he told me about an even deeper frustration with his players. They were not doing their workouts away from the team that they had committed to doing. "They just don't get it!" he complained.

I hear so many people in coaching who demand so much from the people that they lead, yet when we dig into their own lives together, we find it painted with failure, setback, and the inability to stay perfect with commitments. That's not to shame them, that's just the reality of the fact that no one is perfect in how we operate. So why do we demand that of others?

I've been there too. I remember creating our first training manual and I wrote in there that people should do an exercise *every day*. Joshua told me not to write it. I asked why and he said, "Jamie, what do you do consistently, *EVERY DAY* in your life?"

Aside from eating, sleeping, talking, and using the restroom, the answer was, "Nothing."

I was writing something that sounded good, but was really creating a standard that no one can keep. My words were intended to help people, but really they would only destroy. Even if people are doing certain things *every single day*, the danger is that they will find their worth in being perfect in performance.

That's how the avalanche of perfection begins.

Perfection, or the pursuit of perfection, is the poison that is killing our people. Don't talk about it. Don't chase it. Don't demand it, because really, outside of Jesus, it doesn't exist. And guess what, if you *were* perfect, you wouldn't be able to lead me.

Perfection is the enemy of creation. It's the adversary of creativity. It's the greatest foe to your own personal greatness.

What I care about for those I work with and those I am surrounded by is *progress*. It's what I remind myself of regularly, yet still tend to neglect at times. It's making a move towards growth in a certain area trying to not only get better, but actually targeting failure in that area so we can learn what's getting in the way and experiment with finding a creative solution.

It all starts here. Regardless of what you feel, and regardless of what you believe,

You are not your past
You are not your performance
You are not your potential

But how many of us are treating ourselves and others according to those three standards?

Your worth comes from who you are, not what you do, and as we move toward a deeper understanding of that fundamental truth, we can move toward progress and let go of perfection.

Throughout this book and throughout your journey in life, this principle is absolutely imperative to your growth. Every day will present a new challenge, and at least once every week you will experience failure. But what I care about is the growth and pro-gression over the next six months to two years.

I care about the long game. And I care about what it really is, not what it looks like. You should too.

- What kind of things are you demanding of others that you cannot deliver yourself?
- When has the pursuit of perfection undermined your motivation and execution of controllables?
- What are a few areas for growth in which you can start to track progress?

One Percent Better

———

HERE'S THE TRUTH ABOUT PROGRESS: It *cannot* be accelerated.

I think what happens for so many of us is that we want grandiose gains. We want to get 1,000% better in like six or seven areas of our game or our lives *today*. Really, if we're honest, we want to be a million percent better *yesterday*. Let's just say it like it is: We want to be perfect because that's what we think is happening for everyone else who we see on TV, Twitter, Snapchat, and Instagram.

Many of us want these huge gains so that we can feel good about the event or the game or the tournament or whatever we have coming up. We want to feel good about ourselves. But, that's not the way that progress works. In fact, our desire to accelerate growth is actually one of the greatest inhibitors to our personal greatness!

Growth works in small gains. They're one percent gains and they are usually only in a few key areas. Even though everyone can get one percent better each day, most won't. You know why? Because, one percent isn't sexy.

You don't even see one percent most of the time. One percent gains are so marginal that usually you walk away from training and say, "I got the crap beat out of me today," and you totally miss out on how you grew.

I recently knocked four seconds off of a running test after two weeks of hard training. I felt defeated. Even though the results improved, I wanted a bigger improvement because I have this arbitrary standard in my mind of how fast I *should* be able to complete the run. In reality, the four seconds I knocked off my time was a five percent gain.

Simple math:
5% > 0% and 5% > 1%

I speak with many parents, and they all agree that most days, they feel like they got their teeth kicked in by their kids. The house is a mess. Dinner is tasteless and boring. The laundry is not done, and getting to bed was WWIII. Some days we do have big gains. Somedays there is ease and great progress that we readily see. But those days are not *every day*.

Who lowers their stroke average by a stroke each week? Who knocks five seconds off their mile time each run? Who raises kids who never poop in their pants again past the age of three?

Answer: No One

If we're not careful, our pursuit of the extravagant will cause us to miss the unremarkably essential. It's the unremarkably essential gains that really move the needle over time because the gains that really make a difference are so marginal that we often can't see them.

That was the case for the British Cycling Team.

James Clear shares a great story about how the British Cycling Team embraced growth.[5] They created a five-year plan to get better by one percent in a handful of areas: Lighter equipment, more effective nutrition, more efficient training, better sleep, better recovery, and even washing their hands one percent better!

They didn't win the Tour de France in five years; they won it in two! In the end, their willingness to seek the one percent that others neglected, and do it over and over and over, widened the gap between them and their competitors.

It's hard to pursue marginal gains because they are really difficult to see. Because we can't always see the marginal gains and because we are chasing the arbitrary standard of where we *should* be, we have a propensity to try to accelerate growth. When we try to accelerate growth, we miss out on all the little things that we could be learning and accruing that are going to help us sustain greatness later on. We have to slow down to go fast.

.0003% Better

A great friend of mine coaches golf at the division one level and shares a beautiful story about the importance of marginal gains.

Every year we have a banquet for the sports teams where the coaches speak about their respective teams season and give out MVP awards. Its an opportunity to talk up your program, to tell a story or two about some of the kids and to lay out your goals for the next season. The coaches are also asked to talk about the success of their program the year before.

Our golf program had just come off their 2014 season in which we had finished in second place in our conference. It was the highest finish in the history of the program. We broke numerous records as a team and individuals. I looked forward to talking about it.

The evening went as planned. Our kids were congratulated. I spoke about how we had worked hard on our fitness, technique and treating people well. Some coaches that didn't have a great season talked about injuries and changing the culture, the Athletic Director thanked everyone for their hard work.

That evening I laid awake thinking about all I had said and wondering if I had really been authentic about it. What was the real reason for whatever success we had that year? It was then that I realized how most coaches and players actually create their own fairy tale of success and that evening I was pretty much doing the same. People love stories about a new method or culture or training regimen that propelled you to success quickly. Our story wasn't really like that.

Simply, we started the year just trying to get better. The prior year we finished 7th in the league with a team of freshmen and the thought of winning the conference was just a sound bite. We tried to do things in small ways that make you slowly and deliberately better. Unfortunately, I missed out on a great opportunity to talk at our banquet about how small gains can make you great.

The final score from our championship loss was 901-900. The team lamented how each of them could have saved a stroke or two during the event. But how much really separated us from victory? The math says our team needed to be .001% better. Each player only needed to be .0003% better.

What could we have done during the season that would have made each of us slightly better? Writing the small stuff down on paper we soon realized that small gains can occur every day and that some of the small things are extraordinarily small.

I thought about what I could have done as a coach during that tournament to be .001% better. I thought I could have given a better speech before they teed off in the final round. My attempt was sabotaged by my failure to zip my pants, which resulted in hysterical laughing by the entire team, but of course that absorbed the anxiety and ended up being a good thing.

It wasn't until I wrote down all the small things I could have done that I realized it came down to a glaring mistake on my part. I didn't buy the girls the best towels to use for drying their clubs!

During the second round of the tournament a sudden downpour hit and was not predicted by the weathermen. Despite my efforts to tell our players about being prepared only a couple of them had sufficient towels to dry off their grips. In one case, one of the players was using a towel that was less than a foot square, I later accused her of using a napkin to dry her grips. Of course the club came loose in her hand on the ninth hole resulting in a topped shot and the club nearly flying in a lake.

On reflection the whole thing is laughable but accentuates the enormity of the miniscule when it comes to making small gains. The reality is there are many "towel" issues during a season or during a tournament and small gains come in immeasurable ways. Some end up standing out and some never do.

To guess at the start of the season what may be the most important thing to work on or do seems exceedingly difficult. Keep a diary and look at it a couple years later or even the next season. I doubt it ever turns out how you thought but I guarantee that there will always be a small thing you could have done better that in turn makes a large difference.

I later gave a few speeches to booster groups about the value of small gains and how even the smallest of gifts could make a giant difference in the outcome of our season. During the Q and A after these events I get asked by the business folks about my goals for the next season.

What many of them want to hear me say is that we will contend for a title, we will work on our culture and (insert sound bite). I tell them that my goal is to get every player at least .0003% better at a few things and to buy towels for my team.

Getting .0003% better isn't sexy. But it makes a heck of a difference. You don't get .0003% better by writing out goals of what you want to accomplish. You get that little bit better by reflection, introspection, and thinking about controllable commitments.

Again, I don't care what you want. I want to know what you are willing to do to close the gaps between who you are and who you want to become, and where you are and where you want to be.

Don't let your desire for success derail your process in doing the dirty hard work. Don't let your desire to hit the ball better on Thursday undercut your path to greatness. Don't let your desire to win more games this season undercut your growth that will elicit the greatness from your team. Don't let your desire to make your kids well-behaved *now* destroy your relationship and stunt their ability to develop self-control. Don't let the thought of perfection deter you from seeking progress.

There is greatness inside of you, and that greatness will come out one percent at a time.

- What are some areas that you are trying to accelerate in your life?
- What would one percent gains look like in that area?
- What controllable aspects will elicit those gains?
- How long are you going to seek those gains in those areas? (Hint: six months is the shortest timetable I give people I work with.)

- P R I N C I P L E   6 -

Your Personal Greatness

———

SUCCESS IS A WORD THAT's muddled in our culture. Usually success is synonymous with fame or notoriety. It's believed that to be successful we need to have lots of followers, make lots of money, and be well known to millions across the world.

Fame and success are not synonymous. Fame is a by-product, and a fickle one at that. It's an opinion of other people, and opinions sway like leaves in the wind. Success isn't a result. It's an action. As Mark Batterson reminds me, success is doing the best you can, with what you have, where you are.[6]

In order for you to be in the process of *that* success, you need to tap into your personal greatness. Greatness is not fame. It's not a title you receive. It's something inside of you. It's something inside of me. It's something inside of every living person on the planet.

We were all perfectly and meticulously made for a purpose, not just a destination, a certain accolade, title, position, or degree of wealth. We were made for the purpose of connection and creation.

It's been said that we are most like the Creator when we create. We love creation. Watch a three-year old and see the joy on her face as she creates a make believe scenario and immerses herself in it, in a public space! Watch my son JJ make his own Disney World out of a U-Haul cardboard box and a spatula. Watch someone get that buzz of adrenaline as they write an article, play a piece of music, or create a solution to someone's problem.

We love to create. We are born for it. It's what makes us truly come alive. When we can connect with others in the midst of creation, we live a life of passion and purpose. *That* is greatness!!

We all have our own unique experiences. We all have unique ways of influence. We all have unique passions and desires. Sadly, though, our uniqueness is crushed by messages of conformity and fear.

You know this one. There are dreams and desires you have that feel childish when you think about them. *"Come back down to reality right now!!"* you hear screaming loudly at you. Usually, you do. Many of us do. Though it feels like the "right" thing to do, the world suffers from our choice to quiet the unique greatness that we all possess.

Don't limit your greatness for the stability of a check. Jobs can fill your pocket, but dreams will fill your soul.

When I talk of personal greatness, I don't speak of fame. When I talk about uniqueness, I don't mean doing something that no one has ever thought of. Greatness is not originality, because originality comes out of relentlessly stealing like an artist.[7]

Greatness is the ability to free the passions and desires that have been suppressed, embrace them unashamedly, and fan them into flame. Greatness is choosing to live a life uncontrolled by fear and unbridled by what you *should* be doing. Greatness is being responsibly irresponsible.

Greatness requires that we battle perception with truth. The perception is, you are not good enough. The perception is that some are a part of the "chosen few." But the truth is that we are enough, because He is enough. Marianne Williamson's words pierce deeply on the matter of truth vs fear:

> *"Our deepest fear is not that we are inadequate. Our deepest fear is that we are powerful beyond measure. It is our light, not our darkness that most frightens us. We ask ourselves, 'Who am I to be brilliant, gorgeous, talented, fabulous?' Actually, who are you not to be? You are a child of God. Your playing small does not serve the world. There is nothing enlightened about shrinking so that other people won't feel insecure around you. We are all meant to shine, as children do. We were born to make manifest the glory of God that is within us. It's not just in some of us; it's in everyone. And as we let our own light shine, we unconsciously give other people permission to do the same. As we are liberated from our own fear, our presence automatically liberates others."[8]*

Your greatness may never pop up on my twitter feed. Your pursuit of a dream destined to fail without divine intervention may never be captured in a TED Talk. That's not what greatness is about. Greatness doesn't do things for a reward. Greatness finds the reward in the process of creating and connecting. It's living as though the *activity* is the reward, instead of seeking a reward for the activity.

Greatness is what our world needs. Greatness is not something you get or obtain; it's something inside of you that needs to be unearthed. You may not be able to verbalize what that greatness is or what it looks like, but you know what it is deep down inside.

It's what causes you to come alive. It's what gives you great joy. It's what shatters your heart. When you tap into that greatness you have strong moments of connection and purpose.

When you get in the process of creating what you are actually passionate about, your unique greatness will bloom.

None of us know exactly what it will look like or how it will be expressed, but living a life of principles will help you shovel away the muck, and polish your creativity as you engage with what is uniquely you.

Some of you play sports. Some of you teach. Some of you coach. Some of you write. Some of you code. Some of you lead organizations. Some of you parent. I don't care where you are, what you've done, or what you do for a living. Greatness is inside of you, and it takes an insane amount of mental toughness to unearth, embrace, and fan that greatness into flame.

Greatness isn't for the chosen few. Greatness is for the few who choose. It's for the few who consistently make the choice to operate out of love instead of fear. It's for the few who are willing to play long game instead of short game. And it's for the few who consistently choose to live according to principles in the midst of resistance. We all have the ability to choose, and your choice creates your challenge. But your choice creates your chance too.

Everyone I have met who has embraced that uniqueness, who creates and connects with other people, tells me that they meet resistance every day. Creating is difficult, and connecting with others is downright terrifying for many. However, it's the ability to live according to principles regardless of our feelings and circumstances that allows us to live a full and meaningful life.

You were perfectly and meticulously created for a purpose. You have a unique form of greatness inside of you, and you are meant to live in freedom. Your worth doesn't come from what you do; it comes from who you are. Who you are becoming always trumps what you are doing.

So name your principles. Put up the ropes. And start creating.

- P R I N C I P L E   7 -

Fan Your Gifts Into Flame

———

I MET SOMEONE RECENTLY WHO plays basketball at the collegiate level. She was having a tough time on the court that year and in this particular game, she was having a nightmare. Passes were going astray, shots were missing the rim altogether, and she was consistently getting scored on. With each mistake, her impact on the game shrunk smaller and smaller, and she operated with extreme timidity. It looked like she would have paid someone $100,000 just to take her off the court.

She approached me later about one of our books and the effect it's had on her, and I began to engage by asking what she is passionate about. She told me the degree she was pursuing and how she wanted to be a college coach. I never asked what she was studying or what she wanted to be. But usually when people go there they are telling me that they have no passions to pursue or, at least, their passions won't pay the bills. And that was this girl to a T!

"Basketball is all I've ever done and known in my life." I could see that she was falling into the trap of a limited experience.

I don't knock her for not having many other experiences growing up. It's the limiting belief that the future can only be in something that she has experienced and known in the past. We are all in danger of falling into the same trap.

"I'd really love to coach, because then I wouldn't be the one playing. I could just lead from the sideline."

I didn't respond to her comment with words, only with a deeply saddened silence. I wasn't just saddened for her and her feelings of languishing, but for the countless people who are being mentored by folks that want to *just* lead from the sideline. People who want to tell others what to do and tell them to get outside of their comfort zone, without having to model it themselves.

We have this insane notion that the title of captain, coach, boss, president, or parent automatically gives us the ability to influence and affect change. But a title does not equate to followers.

Having a title doesn't mean you have influence, and not having a title doesn't mean you *don't* have influence. Influence isn't gained by achievement or accolades. It isn't attained by having a degree and letters after your name.

Influence is earned through the story you are living. It comes from the life that you have lived to date, and what you are consistently modeling right now. It comes from the fortitude you show in the midst of resistance and struggle.

Simply put, you need to be in the pursuit of following your dreams and scratching towards *your* greatest potential in order for me to follow.

Leadership positions and titles can demand compliance, but they rarely elicit greatness.

THE COURAGE NEEDED TO FAN GIFTS INTO FLAME

One of my favorite passages of Scripture comes in II Timothy 1:6-7. Paul is talking to a young Timothy, maybe 14 to 19 years old, and is not only encouraging him, but admonishing him to fan his gifts into flame. Paul knew that Timothy had the gift of preaching, but there was timidity in Timothy much like the timidity we see in those we get to lead and influence.

It's crazy how we can see the greatness in others that they rarely acknowledge themselves. It's like my friend who was livid with me because I wouldn't shoot more in our soccer game. I took two players on and scored a goal during a tight game, and my friend yelled, "Jamie, why are you messing around?!?! Do more of *that*!!! You can take this game over *if you want to*!"

My friend could see what I had the ability to do, but it was the very thing I was afraid of doing myself. I suppressed the desire to play harder believing that I truly wasn't capable.

I think the same thing was happening with Timothy, and it's likely the same thing is happening with you. Timothy was probably wondering, "*Who am I, as a teenager, to start teaching grown men and women?!"* It was the fear of inadequacy and what others thought that was holding him back.

Paul's admonition was that we *need* you to embrace what you uniquely have. We *need* you to fan your gifts into flame. But it's not easy. That's why the next verse encourages, "God has not given us a spirit of fear, but of power, love, and self-control."

Why does Paul remind him of this? Because it takes *insane* courage to fan your gifts into flame. It takes insane power to demand the ball on the court when you feel like others are angry that you keep shooting. It takes a lot of self-control to quit your job and pursue your passion while leading your family. It takes enormous depths of love to help an enemy who is hurting. Others cannot choose for you. They cannot directly fan your gifts into flame. You have to embrace it and do the dirty hard work yourself.

I've spoken about the concepts in this and other books for years, and I've seen the effect they've had on others. However, I have to be the one who chooses to take those concepts and get them in a book. Writing a book takes self-control and an insane amount of courage, and that's exactly what it takes for you to fan your gifts into flame.

Though he didn't fan Timothy's gifts into flame, Paul played a pivotal role in Timothy's choice. He was sharing what he could see and he was encouraging Timothy to move. But Paul didn't threaten him or shame him. He didn't do what many in leadership roles do in saying, "If you don't do _____ then (insert consequence)." He didn't say, "If you don't do _____ then you are (insert a derogatory term or phrase)."

And for what it's worth, saying these things in your coaches or leaders meetings behind closed doors isn't helping the situation. It's psychologically conditioning yourselves to see and draw out the very things in that person that frustrate you!

Paul didn't push. Paul didn't beg. Paul affirmed Timothy's autonomy.

Notice that Paul didn't say "Let me help you fan your gifts into flame." As leaders and influencers, we cannot directly fan someone's gifts into flame. Timothy, like all of us, had the power to choose. But Paul did play a role in affecting change in Timothy. He went back to a simple truth: God has given you power, love and self-control. He didn't bitch, beg, pull or prod. He said, *this is what it takes to embrace your gifts, these are the things that are yours in Christ, and here is what is true about this situation.*

But here's the thing, Timothy had to hear that from someone who was living it.

Paul was sold out to the mission he believed God gave him. He was unwavering in his belief that God had visited him on the Emmaus road. Even though he was beaten, slandered, and threatened with his life, he was still pursuing a mission that he was willing to die for. It was a dream that was destined to fail without divine intervention. Timothy had experienced Paul's life. He had seen firsthand how Paul was moving forward and embracing the things that scared him, and that's exactly why Paul could help fan that gift into flame.

I wonder what would change if we stopped talking to others about getting out of their comfort zone and invited them to see a life that models it?

It's *our* pursuit of embracing the hardships of growth and development that allows others to link up with us and move forward themselves. It's our progress in the struggle that allows others to genuinely connect with us. It's our engagement with resistance that allows us to empathize with those we get to lead and treat them like people, not production units.

I see far too many people who are trying to lead by piling up stacks and stacks of logs and dry kindling on top of a little spark they see. They hover over people and bombard them with information, quotes, books, and inspirational videos. They smother them with encouragement and sometimes try to do the work for them. They try to cram forty years of life experience into a sixty-minute office meeting and expect their people to accept the information, apply it, learn from it, and thrive.

Sadly, I've been one of those people.

But that's not how growth happens. That's not how people embrace their own personal greatness.

Your personal greatness must be fanned. Like a small ember, it must be blown on gently and consistently. It must not be smothered because it needs air to breathe. It needs the right amount of kindling at the right time for it to catch fire.

Simply put, it needs an optimal environment in which it can grow. And optimal doen't mean easy.

Your words can be the breath of air that meets the ember, but it takes someone embracing their own journey to know that the process cannot be accelerated and they cannot force the fire to grow.

In leadership, we want change now. But leaders who are on the journey themselves know that there is no enduring change that happens right now. There are no fixes or switches that one can flip. As leaders and influencers we can only create an environment ripe for change. And we create that environment by the life that they see, not the words that we say.

Fanning other people's gifts into flame can only come from fanning your gifts into flame - Chasing a dream that is destined to fail without divine intervention. When people see you living that way, you elicit the greatness from others.

"The test of leadership is not to put greatness into humanity, but to elicit it, for the greatness is already there." - James Buchanan

A Few Expectations Are Better Than One

———

WHAT DO YOU DO WHEN you, your team or your organization is having *"one of those days?"*

You know, one of those days when it seems like there is no energy from the time your team shows up. They look lethargic. You're feeling tired too, and you can tell by the way they are joking and laughing that today is going to be a challenge.

Or maybe you start to see mistakes early on in practice. You know, the simple fundamentals that you have gone over thousands of times are sloppy and there seems to be little care.

Or maybe in the office there is a simple drag or lull in the communication. Those you lead aren't responding or interacting with the desired amount of intent and sharpness.

I had somebody who I've worked with for a few years call me. She coaches in college and she experienced one of those days.

I'd just visited the program a week earlier and they had an awesome practice and preparation for their upcoming game. There was high energy, great failure, loud communication, and the coaches had implemented a lot the stuff we had talked about.

I left later that night, they practiced the following day and had a game the next day. They played very well as a team, battled through some adversity, and won the game.

Two days after the game, the coach called me and I said, "It seems like things are going in a pretty good direction." She said, "Jamie, coming off the *best* day of practice we've had all year while you were here, we followed it up with the *worst* day of practice." She said, "Jamie, you wouldn't belieeeeve how frustrated I was!!!"

So, like many of us have, she blew up on the team screaming at them to the point where her assistant coach said, "You know, there were some really good basketball points in there, but I don't think they heard them amidst all the f-bombs you were dropping."

She brought some of the people she considers leaders back in. She said, "We're going to figure this out. What's going on and how are we going to fix it? I want to know what's going on!"

So, three girls stayed quiet, but then the fourth girl, who I'm excited about, because she stood up and spoke from the heart, said, "I don't know what it is, but I know that *your* negativity isn't helping."

Take a second and imagine what your face would look like hearing that in this particular context. Yeah, don't judge the coach. We've all been here.

So, then the coach started seeing red and laid into them even deeper. She got so frustrated and she turned around and started to walk away. Then the last girl said, "So what, you're just gonna walk out on us!? I thought we are a family!"

You can only imagine that it just escalated even further.

On the phone she said, "Jamie, I thought we were past this. I thought we were *past* this. I thought we'd learned our lesson."

I paused and said, "Honestly, I thought *you and I* were past this."

I said, "For two years, we've been working on you. You've been training and learning to adapt and use your emotions instead of letting your emotions use you. We've been working on these things for *two years*, and I've got to be honest, I thought *you* were past this."

I didn't say this to shame her, because shame never equips. I'll say it again, *SHAME NEVER EQUIPS!!!* I said this to highlight the fact that most of the time it's our expectations that get in the way.

I said, "When I look at you, I have two expectations. I have the expectation that you're going to be fantastic. That you're going to implement all the things that you've learned and you're going to treat people like people regardless of what happens. You're going to absorb anxiety and be phenomenal.

But, I also have the expectation that you're going to get pissed and you're going to lose it. Why? Because I know that you're human and you're not perfect in your behavior. I know that *I* don't just learn *my* lesson one time and then never err in that manner again. In fact, most of us don't in many aspects of our lives."

Expecting to learn from a mistake and *never* make that mistake again is an insane standard in most contexts in our lives. I don't live that way across the board, and I'm willing to bet that you don't either. So why should we expect that from other people?

I said, "Really, what we need to have is a few expectations. If you really want to be able to adapt to a situation, you need to have many expectations. You need to fully expect that the people that you are leading are going to take the information and grow from strength to strength. But, you also need to fully expect that they're going to come in with low energy some days. They're going to forget basic things you have covered. It's going to get ugly. There are going to be setbacks and bouts of frustration. And people are flat out going to get things wrong. You have to build in for that and make sure that you are not demanding perfection. By all means have high standards, just don't have ridiculous ones like perfection."

It's amazing how quickly we can be derailed when our reality doesn't meet our expectations.

It's like the guy who plays professional golf getting upset because the green didn't break the way it's *supposed to*. What person on this earth determines the way a hole *should* break?! It breaks the way it breaks! If you missed the putt, you need to adapt, learn, and move forward. Or don't, and get frustrated at the course and watch your level of play rapidly diminish.

It's the same with ourselves, our people, families, and organizations. You cannot say how a season, fiscal year, a practice, or even a day is *supposed* to go. You can have an idea and plan according to that idea, and you should. But the spoils are for those who are able to adapt when reality does not meet expectations.

It's the way that the military and the law enforcement train. When they get ready for a mission, or for anything that they're going into, they don't just run through their *one* plan of how they think things will happen. They run through all sorts of contingencies preparing to adapt, not if, but *when* things go crazy. They totally expect that plans and expectations will fly out the window the minute a round is fired. They're not caught off guard by it. They are ready to adapt and execute.

I wonder what would happen if we didn't cling to just one expectation, but instead carried at least two? Then I wonder what would happen if instead of dwelling on our expectations and worrying about how things will go we focused our energy towards principles we want to execute?

What areas of your life consistently go wayward? If you have a family, then you know the great little Saturday you have planned can turn into a trip the hospital, an emotional melt down, or an emergency trip to the store for new underwear.

I know that in your job there can be what you have scheduled, and then what you get thrown at you by your team or boss.

I know that in your sport you can have world-class preparation, but when the game comes, the officials, opposing team, your shot, or your teammates can all miss the mark of what you expected. How do you adapt?

The answer lies in practicing the ability to pivot in various situations throughout your life.

There is an old adage that "We need to expect the best and prepare for the worst." There is some wisdom in that statement, but I have seen many people who end up preparing for the worst and then bring out the worst in their teams or themselves due to their anxiety and stress on fixing things. I would argue that we need to expect the best *and* expect the worst, but we focus on executing in both.

Your expectations will be crushed. There is no choice in that. But your adaptability is always a choice.

- What expectations do you have for your team or organization that consistently frustrate you and others in leadership?
- I wonder if your team's inconsistency is modeled by your inconsistency in handling pressure or challenging situations?
- What expectations do you have for yourself? Are they expectations according to an arbitrary standard of what you think you should be able to do?
- What would multiple expectations look like for you, your family, and your team?

Surrender The Results

———

I HAD THE PLEASURE OF meeting and absorbing wisdom from a guy who served as a Navy SEAL. There were many stories he told that resonated with me that day.

Like when he said that he had to pass a fifty-meter swim without surfacing. He went into that swim knowing that he had to pass to enter the next level of training, while also knowing that he could not make the fifty meters underwater. The only way he could make it to the next stage was if he chose not to surface.

He smiled, and said, "I didn't come up."

That's right, he knowingly went into that test with the plan of passing out underwater!

That was crazy. But that's not the most important story he told. The most important thing he said was:

"The only time you can operate with complete self-control in live battle is when you do not care what they do to you."

In essence, you don't care if you get shot, burned, tortured or anything else. When you have surrendered the results, then, and only then, can you operate with self-control.

I've never been in a war setting so please know that I am not saying this is easy. But he spoke about it as though it's something as regular as spreading butter on toast.

Of course he would rather live than die. He had a wife and young kids. He had ambitions in life beyond his military career. But he didn't let his desire to live cloud his focus on execution. The moment that he focuses on just staying alive is the very moment that he takes his eye off the process. If he was thinking about the result he would not be present executing the details of his team's mission. If he is dwelling on questions of how the future will work out, that's when someone is likely to get hurt.

It's not that the results don't matter. They do. You just can't control them.

When we shift our focus to the process instead of entertaining anxious thoughts about the outcome, we will be surprised at what we can accomplish. It's a very simple truth: the best results come surrendered.

Stop Talking About It

I get to work with a guy who plays professional golf. Let's call him James. James used to play on the PGA Tour, but now plays on the Web.com tour, which is basically the league below the PGA.

When I started walking alongside James he was in pursuit of winning enough to make it back to the main tour. To get on the PGA tour, you get your "tour card." I heard a lot about this card on our calls together. In order to get his *card* he had to earn money by placing in tournaments. To earn money, he had to play well enough to *make the cut* two days into a four-day tournament. Guys who shot low enough to stay in the tournament for the last two days could make money bringing them closer to securing their card.

With that being said, what two phrases do you think habitually came out of James's mouth every call? That's right: *"Gotta make the cut"* and *"Gotta get my card."*

What do you think happened the more he focused on making the cut and getting his card? That's right, he missed a bunch of cuts and moved further away from the desired outcome.

Needing results weirdly seems to push desired outcomes further away. I'm sure you've seen a guy who is absolutely crazy about a girl and wants to date her so badly that he does some really weird things. He tries to be deeply romantic but it comes off as being a creepy stalker. His need to have her causes him to be inauthentic and do dumb stuff. And essentially, he pushes her further and further away. (By the way, ladies, you do this too!)

The same thing happened for my friend James. Every day playing golf became so important that he placed unnecessary stress on himself and took his eye off of controllables. Every shot became a "What if?" You know, that crazy little road we go down where one mistake can set off a chain reaction of unfortunate events that will leave us flailing in life.

What if I miss this shot? Then I probably won't get a birdie. Then I won't make the cut. Then I won't get my Tour Card. Then I won't be playing alongside my friends. Then I won't make money. Then I'll lose my car, my house, and all of the things I need to live. And then.... You get the picture and you know how it goes. That line of thinking sucks!

After a tournament where he played poorly, I decided something needed to change. James needed to surrender the results. It's one thing to see what other people need. It's another to model it for them. I had to model it. So we got on the phone and I asked some questions.

"James, if you knew you weren't going to get your card at the end of this season, but you knew you would get it at the end of the following season, how do you think things would change?"

He got really quiet and there was that nervous pause on the other end of the phone.

"Well, yeah, things would be a lot different," he said.

Now, I could tell, and he confirmed it later, that uttering those words felt like he was giving up and lying down. You see, the fear is that when we stop thinking or worrying about the results, then we might not have the right motivation to continue moving forward. If there is no prize at the end, will we still work hard?

I wasn't asking him to give up on pursuing his dream. I was asking him to give up what was holding him back. It was his focus on *achieving* the dream that kept him from *pursuing* the dream and scratching his potential.

I see this way too often with parents and people in coaching where their care actually comes off as control. They want their kids to be happy, affirmed, and successful. Ironically, though, the thing they want most for their kids is impeded by the thing *they* need most for themselves: the results of their kids being happy, affirmed, and successful.

"How do you think you would handle a bad shot if and when it happens next week?" I asked.

"I probably wouldn't slam my club or get pissed at myself or my caddy. I'd try to learn from what I did so I don't consistently make the same mistake in the future." he said.

"That's right, James, and if you consistently learn from mistakes and grow from each round, what do you think will happen over the next twelve months?"

"I'll be in a much better place and probably playing much better golf," he admitted.

"So here's the thing, James. I'm not going to work with you if you are going to continue to talk about your *Tour Card* because even if you do get your card this year, you will be in the same place next year on the PGA Tour chasing cuts and focusing on results.

Your character won't have changed and your experience will be the same. I honestly believe that the best thing for you, is that you play on the Web.com tour next year if, and only if, we work on who you are becoming."

Silence.

I knew saying those words increased the likelihood that I would no longer have a client. But I also knew that it was the best thing for him. Although I could help him cope and get better, the root of the pain would not cease unless he was willing to surrender the result.

What did I really want? I wanted him to succeed *and* I wanted to keep a client. But in trying to keep a client I wouldn't allow him to succeed. I needed to model surrendering results.

"James, if we are going to work together, we are going to start living a mission instead of chasing a goal. We are going to pursue excellence in golf, and if we do that, I believe that the results will probably be even better than what you could imagine, but we have to start focusing on the controllables. Are you in?"

To his credit, James did what many other people I've worked with were unwilling to do. He embraced it and is still living that mission. I rarely hear those two phrases come out of his mouth. Guess what's happening to his stress levels? And guess what's happening to the results? As I finish this book, he is back on the PGA Tour and has radically transformed his character.

"WHAT IF" TO "EVEN IF"

Here is a simple shift that I encouraged James to make. It's one that I think will serve you well. It's moving from the thought *What if* to *Even if*. Instead of thinking "What if?" and then listing out all of our doomsday scenarios, we can prepare for likely mistakes or setbacks moving to "Even if" and deciding how we will move forward in a beneficial manner.

Instead of James thinking, "What if I don't get my tour card?" he moved to "*Even if I don't get my tour card,* I will learn about how much more important scoring is than being the top in driving distance."

Instead of James thinking, "What if I don't hit this green?" he moved to "*Even if I don't hit this green,* I will learn from my swing and learn how to let go of poor shots. I will choose to focus on the principles in my chipping and get the ball close to the hole."

That is not only a new way of thinking, it's a new way of living. It's giving us back the clarity and self-control needed to keep moving forward in living our mission.

I wonder what would happen if you started to surrender results in your life? I wonder what results you need to surrender?

I don't know if the book you are writing is going to sell millions of copies. In fact, most don't. Most people who write had to write multiple books before one had a huge impact on the world. But if you are trying to write the next *Harry Potter, Purpose Driven Life,* or *7 Habits of Highly Effective People,* then you are likely to write something that sucks. I know that's blunt, but it's probably true.

Here is a much better place: "*Even if* my book sells only three hundred copies I will have refined my writing, exercised self-control in using time and managing emotions, and I may have touched one life in the process."

Instead of dwelling on "What if I don't start this year for my team?" which you cannot control, let's move here: "*Even if* I don't start this year, I will choose to work on my communication and the ability to hone in on the present instead of listening to myself."

Instead of focusing on "What if my team doesn't make the post-season?" let's move to "*Even if* we don't make the post-season I'm going to hold high standards and boundaries, I'm going to develop better body language for my team, and I am going to work on treating people according to who they are, not what they do."

Instead of focusing on "What if I don't get into the college I want?" let's move to "*Even if* I don't get into the college I want, I will choose to read and study the people who are in my desired field, I will learn how to ask questions of people who do what I want to do, and I will develop maybe *the* most important skill in life: resourcefulness."

This is not an exercise in being positive. It's not about finding the silver lining in situations. And it's not letting yourself or others off of the hook. Yes you need to surrender the results; but you cannot surrender the resposibility.

This is an exercise in shifting our focus from uncontrollables to controllables. It's about doing what's most beneficial instead of being persuaded by fears and challenges of our circumstances. It's about regaining some sense of control in the fight. And the resposibility of controlling controllables is actually harder than just talking about and focusing on results.

When we surrender results, then we can operate with self-control. It provides the mental and emotional clarity to focus on the things that actually drive the results. It allows us to work with poise and discipline to think and act clearly and swiftly. And in teams and organizations, it gives us the ability to interact with people in a way that absorbs their anxiety and allows them to fan their gifts into flame.

Surrendering results is not giving up on a dream. It's not giving up in the fight. It's giving up what is getting in the way of you scratching your greatest potential.

- Can you remember a time when your focus on results pushed the results further and further away?
- If you could do it over again, how would you have done it differently?
- What results do you dwell on that you know you need to surrender?
- If and when you surrender them, what controllables do you need to focus on that will likely bring the best results?
- Most importantly, who do you want to become as you pursue that dream?
- Even if your year or season doesn't meet expectations, who will you become and what effect will you have on others?

Confidence vs. Conviction

———

THE NUMBER ONE THING PEOPLE say they lack and desperately need to excel is confidence.

Confidence is extremely misunderstood and, in my opinion, way overrated. Why? Because confidence is a feeling we derive from the interpretation of other feelings, circumstances, and the likelihood of future results.

If you've ever played golf then you know this one. You can be striping shots on the range before you play, shaping the ball however you want, and feel great or *confident* about your round. But then you get out on the course and start spraying the ball everywhere.

I'm amazed at how many people in top-level golf affirm that the opposite happens frequently: when they have little control of the ball on the range, they tend to play well on the course.

But wait a minute. If you didn't have feelings of confidence from your time on the range, how did you start playing well on the course? This is where confidence is fickle.

When I hear people talk about confidence, they usually use the language that they *lost* their confidence. As though it's something that can be misplaced or, worse yet, taken away from you. This leads people towards chasing confidence like a feather in the wind. They spend so much time trying to *feel* a certain way instead of operating according to principles. And this is where people become stuck and powerless.

And another thing, if you don't have confidence now, where do you get it? Most people will say from past results. And that's true. Having success on stage during past speaking events *can* help me feel confident. But what if you don't have many great results in the past to spring forward from, what do you do?

There has to be a better way, and there is. We need to speak less about confidence and focus more on operating with conviction.

Confidence and conviction are similar, yet very different.

Dictionary definitions of confidence are:

- A feeling or belief that you can do something well or succeed at something
- The feeling of being certain that something will happen or is true
- A feeling of reliance on one's circumstances

Notice the common themes. It's a *feeling* and it's usually tied to the certainty of a result in the future or the likelihood of a great result because of circumstances. And this is where confidence is a slippery slope. No one knows what the results are going to be regardless of what strategy you employ. No one can tell you how things are going to work out. If you could control results you would be the highest paid commodity in the world. But you can't.

Don't get me wrong; confidence is a real thing. There is no doubt about it. But when someone feels confident, they usually are not experiencing thoughts about what other people think or how things are going to pan out for them in the future. That's what we really want when we talk about finding confidence. We want those moments of clarity where we are not thinking about things around us. Those moments happen, but they are not always the norm. We don't always have that level of clarity or assurance.

When Vanderbilt dropped our soccer program, my dad didn't say *everything will be okay and work out.* He circled to principles: we will pray and we will move to next steps.

When our bible college was in danger of not getting funded, our Head Master pointed us back to principles: we will pray about it, God is the provider, and focus on your studies.

There were no promises of how things would turn out. But there was an unwavering belief that those principles and truths were tried, tested, and true. And that's the beauty of conviction; there is no tie to how things will turn out. Conviction is the state of being fully convinced that your *process* is optimal, and it's the act of fully committing to your strategy and beliefs, regardless of how you feel. When we are convicted in executing on our principles, we often begin to operate with greater clarity.

CONVICTION IN YOUR PROCESS

James Clear shares a great story of a guy named Trent Dyrsmid. At the age of 23 Trent began working as a stockbroker. Within eighteen months, he had built up a $5 million book of business with a simple strategy. Everyday he came to work with two cups. One was empty. The other had 120 paper clips in it.

Each day, Trent would get on the phone with prospects and after every call he would move one paper clip over to the empty cup. He didn't leave his desk until all 120 paperclips were in the other cup. He did this for the better part of two years, and the results speak for themselves.[9]

Was Trent's process terribly complicated or difficult? No.

Was it the *best* strategy? Who knows.

But one thing is for certain; Trent was completely committed to the process. And that's the crux of conviction. Conviction is being strongly persuaded or certain of what you believe to be true. It's being fully convinced that the strategy you are committing to is a great strategy and embracing it even in the face of setback and staggering results.

It's *not* a feeling of assurance in how things are going to pan out. It's a conscious choice in attitude and focus as you move forward right now. It's an unwavering commitment to principles that you believe will elicit the greatest impact and best results.

I'm sure Trent had plenty of days where no one wanted to talk with him. I'm sure that there were long stretches where it seemed like things were stagnating. And I'm sure there were stretches of significant gain where he had made a few million dollars and at those times it would have been easy to change strategies.

But that's part of it. Had he done that for only one month, he might not have seen much of a return. The same way that people want to practice a jump shot for three days and suddenly shoot like Steph Curry. That's not training. That's looking for a fix. That's looking for that bit of pixie dust that will elicit the feeling of confidence because if we can *feel* confident, we believe everything else will change.

Feelings of confidence *can* bring about an assurance that allows us to fully operate according to principles. But confidence doesn't guarantee anything. And if you don't feel confident, there is hope for you. You can still choose to operate with conviction just like Trent. The crux of the matter, is that we are decisive. And sometimes it's more important to be decisive than it is to be right.

- What are you decisive about?
- What are some principles that you totally believe are sound and true and will help you close the gap as you commit to them fully and consistently?
- Who do you know who operates with conviction?
- When have you done so yourself?

Though convictions can be strong, operating with conviction does not eradicate feelings of fear. But as you'll see in the next chapter, it chooses to move forward despite of them.

Leave The How To Him

———

HAVE YOU EVER WANTED SOMETHING so bad that it actually hurt? This was one of those times for me.

I was in Ireland trying to secure a work permit to stay in the country. I had just joined a church family and loved them so dearly that I couldn't imagine life with anyone else, anywhere else. My struggle was that my visitor's visa in the country was about to expire, meaning I would have to return home to the states.

Like with many deep desires, I tried to figure out how to make it work, and I launched in on my plan without any reflection, and certainly without the counsel of others who were brighter and older than myself.

I tried to leave the country on a ferry and renew my ninety days on my visitor's visa. That was a bust!

I tried to fly to Brussels to get a fresh stamp on my passport. That worked, or at least I thought at the time.

I tried to get a work permit signing with a pro soccer team. That failed too.

Finally, I found a school that I really loved. It was the Irish Bible Institute. I spoke with family and my pastor Tony about it and then inquired. The school was amazing! The people I met blew me away and I was certain, as certain as one can be, that this is where God wanted me.

The best part of it was that by going to school full time I could work for twenty hours a week. That meant I could play pro soccer too! The stars were aligning, and I started to hear the Black Eyed Peas signing, "I've got a feeling..."

So I got the paperwork filled out and headed to immigration headquarters to get my stamp as a student.

I had been there before and it's a very unpleasant place. People speaking forty different languages, all accompanied with their peculiar smells, are herded like cattle. Some yelling, some crying, and others who looked like they had lived there for the last ten days.

My last few visits didn't go so well but I was confident that this one was different. Remember, confidence is a fickle feeling usually tied to the hope or assurance of a result. But confidence means very little in situations like this. Because confidence can cloud our judgment, keep us from executing our principles, and stain our character in the process.

When I got to the window and handed the lady my paperwork, she flew through it. She asked for her boss, whispered in his ear, and then he turned to me with a smile: "Mr. Gilbert, how about you come around to the back and we will get you all sorted out."

"The back?" I thought. "I've never seen anyone go back there. As an American, it's about time I get some preferential treatment!"

I know that sounds bad and arrogant, but that's *exactly* what I thought.

Well the preferential treatment ended up being me in a little white room with two officers who interrogated me for two hours!

They grilled me with question after question of my intentions in coming to Ireland. Suddenly my goal, my aim, my hope, and my assumption of God's will were at stake. So I panicked. I got away from my principles and lied.

You see, you cannot come into the country and try to get seen by a soccer club. You have to be invited. So I made up a story of playing pick up soccer with a guy who told me I was good. Then he said I should come train with his team. And that team in turn offered me a contract. It was the biggest hunk of made up crap one could scheme.

The only thing true about it was that it was a lie. Flat out.

After two hours of questions and make believe, the officials finally said, "Alright, we don't believe your story, but we cannot prove you're lying. Either way, there is another problem. The school you want to study at is not recognized as a college eligible for foreign students. So, you have two weeks for your school to get accredited by the national board of education and if it doesn't happen in two weeks, you'll have to go home."

Two weeks!? You can't get money out of an ATM in two weeks in Ireland!

It was done in my mind. The barrier felt like a steel door without a handle. Yeah God is big, but this might be *too* big. My mentor Mark Batterson says that more hurt is done to people and God's kingdom because we reduce the size of our God to the size of our biggest problems.[10] That's exactly where I was.

More than that, why would God open the door after what I just did?

I went down a serious road of doubt and self-inflicted guilt that left me feeling useless, unloved, and unlikely to be in Dublin. That's exactly where the devil wants to get us. He wants to get us asking questions. He wants us to grab onto the seed of doubt. He wants us to accept our thoughts as truth. And if we are not careful, we will end up listneing to the lies and nonsense in our heads instead of sowing truths about who God is and who we are.

So for two weeks I worked on getting everything I needed together. The school was working on the accreditation, but it wasn't looking promising. I got my mentor Tony to serve as my sponsoring family in case things fell through financially or I had an emergency during my studies. And I prayed.

But the desire to get that result held my heart so tightly that I still tried to control things. I remember very clearly asking Tony to write a required letter of sponsorship. After reading what he drafted, I asked him to word a sentence in such a way that was misleading at best. Kind of like responding to your mom's question of , "Did you clean your room?" with "I did everything in my power to use all the energy I was willing to invest to clean my room." As I said, misleading at best.

I'll never forget Tony looking at me after my ridiculous request, tipping his glasses down and saying, "Jamie, I'm not going to lie."

It was definitive and loving at the same time. He saw right through me. And that boundary changed much for me. Tony modeled what it looked like to follow Christ. Being truthful, being honest, and not trying to force God's hand to match my agenda. To follow Christ means that we surrender the results. It means that we do not try to figure it all out. We simply follow. But if I'm dead honest, following Christ does not feel totally comforting in every circumstance.

That night, I was in bed with tears running down my face. The tears weren't because I had sinned or done wrong. They weren't because Tony thought ill of me. They were tears that came from conviction. I was totally committed to telling the truth to the officers in our next meeting, and telling the truth meant I wouldn't be in control.

In fact, telling the truth was the *one* thing that could send me packing. I learned that day that we might not always know God's agenda, but we know his will: that we walk in christlikeness.

So I resolved to tell the truth, no matter what. That's a simple principle, but not always easy to do. But that's the case with *any* principle. What is best for us and others is often at war with what we feel, what we want, and what it looks like we need to do to make things happen.

The strategy sounded ridiculous, but I was convicted of three things: God is in control and will get me where He wants me, lying is not how I want to live, and I have a choice in what words come out of my mouth.

If they asked me one more time for my story I would tell them the truth about my intentions in coming over. That was *my* choice. And that's the crux of conviction. It's a choice. Regardless of how you feel, you choose how you are going to operate. And simply choosing to operate accroding to principles does not guarantee that we will get the outcome we want. My choice was to give up control and be honest.

Giving up control is awkward. It brings you to a place of vulnerability and being unsure. But it also brings you to a place of freedom. Like Bob Goff says, when you are with someone you trust, you don't have to know all of the details.[11] And not carrying the burden of knowing it all is a lightness that cannot be adequately described.

It was the first time I remember in my life where I surrendered the outcome. Yeah I cared to stay in Ireland, but I knew that care could not control me. It could only affect me.

So I did the worst case scenario exercise: what's the worst that can happen if I tell the truth? The worst case scenario was not that I would be put in prison, tortured or killed. The worst case scenario was that I would go back to Oklahoma, have a warm bed, drive my own car, be with Amy, be in a reasonable climate and eat Mexican food.

That was a helpful exercise in perspective. But honestly, even after that exercise, I still wanted my result. And I still had to choose how I would operate.

I showed up for my appointment the next morning and the officer from the little white room greeted me and asked if we could step outside. "Great," I thought, "At least they can't do anything to me out in public!"

The man lit up a cigarette, blew out the smoke and said, "Jamie, I'm sorry to say this, but your paperwork for your school hasn't come through yet, and it looks like..." Immediately his phone started ringing. He answered it while I sat there praying on the inside.

The officer's face went blank. He closed his phone starring at a spot off in the distance, stunned. He took another puff, blew it out and said, "Well, that was the office upstairs and they said your school just sent over the accreditation. So... I guess you're free to start your studies."

I wanted to dance. I wanted to cry. I wanted to shout and give him a hug! But the *last* thing I wanted to do was open my mouth and say something that would change his verdict!

So I bottled it up, nodded, went inside, and got my immigration card.

I remember walking along the River Liffey stunned. I did everything in my power to disqualify myself from being in the country. I came over illegitimately. I tried to cheat the system. And I flat out lied to peoples' faces.

But God is not the image that many of us hold. He's not hiding behind a bush with a hammer waiting for us to mess up just so that he can jump out when we do and say, "Caught ya!"

God is a father that unashamedly opens up his arms to embrace us when we turn back to him. He wants the best for us. Much like me with my son, He holds us to certain standards but treats us with grace when we fail saying, "I knew you would fail, I knew you would return, and I know you can learn." That's a different image.

That experience didn't change everything *for* me, but it did change much *about* me. It stands as an experiential lesson in the power of conviction. Though I face many uncertainties about how things will pan out in life, I always have the choice of how I am going to move forward. And you do too.

I've learned that gazing into the future trying to figure out how it will all come together is time and energy wasted. In fact, it is time and energy that is used only to create anxiety and take our focus away from simple things we can steward that will actually close the gaps for us.

We cannot figure it all out, and we don't know how things are going to come together. But we don't have to have it all figured out to keep moving forward. We can be diligent in deciding what principles to adhere to and we can move forward with an unwavering focus on executing those principles regardless of how we feel.

Leave the *how* to Him. Choose your principles. Move forward with conviction regardless of whether or not you feel confident that you will get your intended result. You might just find that what happens is better than you could have imagined.

- What results are you trying to control right now?
- What are simple principles that you can stick to that will increase the likelihood of the result and impact?
- If someone else were in your situation, how would you counsel them on moving forward? We can usually see other people's situations in 20/20 and usually we need to heed the advice we share with them.
- Have you ever felt God carry you through a situation or season in life? If so, reflect on that moment now. If not, he's still here with arms wide open. And I am too. Jamie@ traintobeclutch.com

See People. Not Performance.

———

TAKE OUT SOMETHING TO WRITE on and answer this question: "What is the one message that plays over and over in your head, that you would shut off if you could?"

We will use this later.

Sarah grew up playing youth soccer in the Midwest and was fast becoming one of the best players in her state. She was playing in the state tournament against a rival team and winning by three goals. So she came out of the game to rest her legs and sat down on the bench, which wasn't a very familiar place for her.

On the opposing team there was a girl named Jen who was being highly recruited by a couple different top-level colleges. During the run of play Sarah's coach made a comment that radically affected Sarah's life.

You see Jen had just gotten the ball at her feet and instead of making a simple pass she gave the ball away to the other team. Sarah's team went down and scored. Sarah's coach turned around to the bench and simply said, "See, she's not as good as everyone thinks she is. She's not a gamer."

Some people might think this gave Sarah relief because she was actually better in her coach's eyes than Jen. But the opposite happened. In fact, two things happened. First, every single time the coach said something to Sarah she always thought, "Yeah, but what are you saying about me when I can't hear you?"

Second, through her coach's comment she realized that what really matters is whether or not somebody in authority believes that you're a gamer. Apparently, making mistakes means you're not.

She spent the rest of her life playing soccer trying to live up to an arbitrary standard and being beat down every single time she played because she never felt like she was good enough.

We asked a simple question in one of our workshops recently: "What is the one message that plays over and over in your head, that you would shut off if you could?"

Take a second and look back to what you wrote at the beginning of the chapter. How does it correlate with the answers people listed below?

Here are the answers:

- "You should be on the LPGA. You never scratched the surface of your talent." (She said this was a message from her dad)

- "I am a failure if people see me make a mistake."
- "You're not good enough at this level."
- "You failed in the past and you'll never make that up or be forgiven because no one will forget."
- "You suck."
- "You're not worthy. You're too fat."
- "I am not good enough at _____."
- "If you aren't winning you are failing."
- "I am physically broken."
- "You're worth comes from what you do and what the people you influence do."
- "I'm a fraud. I am not nearly good enough to be in the role I am in."
- "I'll never *arrive*."
- "You're thoughts are *out there*. You need to be more realistic."
- "You are not enough."
- "Am I good enough?"
- "You are not doing enough. You shouldn't be relaxing."
- "I need to earn more to satisfy my expectations and have security."
- "How does everyone feel about the work that I did?"

I want you to know that the people who shared this are all working well-paying jobs, range from twenty-six to fifty-seven years old, most are in leadership positions, and come from every corner of the United States.

Kent Hoffman finds in his research over decades on the subject that the number one message playing in their head that people would shut off if they could is the message of *not enough*.[12]

It's simple. But it's scary. Why?

Because the idea of *not enough* is one of the most common phrases in leadership.

Enough With *Enough*

Before I got on stage to speak with the entire college athletic department at the school-year kick off, they played a video. It showed short clips of hits, goals, sprints, swims, spikes, etc with one message:

> A lot of goals scored, but not enough.
> A lot of races won, but not enough.
> A lot championships won, but not enough.

Then I got up and spoke for two hours on how damaging that message is and how to break free from it! Good thing I have many expectations when I go to speak.

It's a simple reality in life: The majority of us are finding our value in what we do, have done, or could do in the future. This is what makes every at-bat, every pass, every practice, every shot, and every event a test of who we are. People are not just swinging to hit the ball; they are swinging to stay alive.

In order for us to break free from seeing ourselves according to our own performance we have to see people according to who they are. The measure we use to judge other people is often the same measure we use to judge ourselves. Similarly, the measure others use to judge us are the same measures we use to judge ourselves.

When ESPN or sports analysts talk about someone being a genius, talented, or the G.O.A.T, they do so because of performance. What young kids and older kids soon infer is that their worth comes from how well they perform.

When a teacher praises someone in front of the class for winning the regional math competition, *with ease,* many others in the class develop their sense of worth from how they do in comparison to their peers. Not only is comparison the thief of all joy, it's the thief of freedom and creativity.

Instead of praising the result, praise them for their effort, relentlessness, self-discipline and any other process-oriented things that led them to the result. But when we talk about people according to their accomplishments, that's where they, we, and everyone else start to find our worth and value.

Eye Contact
It may sound really simple, but seeing people visually may be the first step to take in treating people like people. I mean actually acknowledging their presence in front of you by stopping to look them in the eye.

I remember Eugene Cho talking about living on Skid Row in L.A.[13] According to Eugene, the hardest thing about living on the street wasn't the fact that he didn't have regular food and sustainable shelter. It was that when everyday people like you and I would walk past him, we wouldn't look him in the eye. Over time he started to feel like little more than an inanimate object.

He felt like he was a fire hydrant or a tree according to everyone else. That was the hardest thing playing on his mind.

Too often we overlook the importance of making eye contact with somebody. Just the simple desire to be seen hits at the heart of our greatest longings and deepest needs. I remind people constantly on Twitter, that people really crave two things: To be authentically heard or seen, and to experience unconditional love.

Use Words Only If Necessary

St. Francis of Assisi once said, "It is no use walking anywhere to preach unless our walking is our preaching." That always challenged me when I was in Bible college. But it also excited me. Who wants to listen to someone who isn't living what they teach?

It has also struck me that the people I learn the most from do little talking. We will benefit greatly in leadership, across the board, if we reduce what we say by asking more questions.

But when you do choose to use words, start here. The most impactful statement that anybody can hear according to studies is,

I love to watch you _____.

I love to watch you play.
I love to watch you jump.
I love to watch you sing.
I love to hear your voice.

Make sure that you insert something that is not results oriented like *I love to watch you win, dominate, birdie, or close a deal.* Make sure you point them back to a controllable part of the process.

Here's the kicker: when you're saying that you love to watch somebody do something or you love just being around them, you're not tying your love to a result according to their performance.

Peter Bregman argues that our appreciation of someone needs to come with no strings or demands attached. "The more someone feels appreciated without the pressure to perform, the better they'll perform."[14] This isn't a strategy. That's just the byproduct of treating people like people.

I'm exhausted from interacting with organizations and people who are struggling because they feel like every move they make is being judged, scrutinized, and will somehow determine the entire trajectory of their lives. I'm heartbroken that grown men can walk to the foul line feeling like their relationship with their dad is hanging in the balance. I'm tired of a sports and business culture that wields the fear of *enough* to drive sales and performance.

We need to get back to truth in order for our world to allow people's creative genius to flow. This is the most fundamental truth:

You are not your past
You are not your performance
You are not your potential

When you treat people like people, you can finally treat yourself like a person: perfectly created, yet being perfected.

- What are some of the measures you use to judge other people?
- Do you measure yourself in the same manner?
- When have you been treated according to your performance?
- Who are five people you can go and appreciate tomorrow without any strings attached?

Talk To Yourself – Don't Just Listen

————

I WAS A HOT SUMMER afternoon in Denver, and I was the only one working out. I was out doing a tough thirty-minute interval run by myself. In this run I'm not trying to cover a particular amount of ground in a certain amount of time, but I am trying to run as hard as I can during each segment when I'm told to sprint. You don't really pass this type of run. You just go until exhaustion. Passing out, throwing up, or dying are really the benchmarks for this workout.

That day I was working extremely hard and I really broke through a few barriers. My lungs were burning and my legs were hurting, but every time I got tired I simply ran harder. It was a great workout to say the least, but when I finished and was bent over gasping for air, the thoughts that hit me sounded like this:

"Jamie, I bet Shane would have done that run better."
"I bet Tyson would have covered more ground and he wouldn't be as tired as you are."
"You barely got through that workout."

"Your face was showing the struggle the whole time and guys who are fit don't look like that when they run."

"Jamie, all the guys in the league would have done better than you."

It took me a few seconds to really acknowledge and hear those thoughts. Then I just laughed. I just did all of that work at a very high level, and then I tried to undercut everything I did!

I remember hearing a story of a guy who completed six double triathlons in his mid-fifties.[15] When asked how he did it, he said that he learned early on that he had to talk to himself instead of just listen.

If he listened to the thoughts in his head, he would have heard all of the reasons why he couldn't do it: *"You're old. You don't have an expert team around you. You're not from Kenya. You don't have worldclass training facilities,"* etc.

His principle hit home for me. The thing about my thoughts that day was that they were not based on facts. They were false constructs or stories that came out of nowhere! Lies! Lies! Lies!

Of course, the guys who do this run show signs of fatigue. If they run it *as hard as they can,* then by the very definition of exhaustion, they would be fatigued! Could they have run further or faster than I did?

Yes. Maybe.

But that wasn't what I was hearing.

We all have crazy thoughts that swirl through our head. Remember, thoughts do not have power. It's only when we click on the thought and zoom into it, accepting it as true, that we give it power over us.

It's true that we can and need to grow in our ability to let thoughts pass by in our minds. But it's also imperative that, like the guy running triathlons, we are intentionally filling our minds with beliefs that are beneficial, life-giving, and true.

I Am Becoming

One of the main reasons you are reading this book and have heard about Train To Be Clutch stems back to a choice Joshua made years ago. He was working with three kids who lived in the Watts Housing projects in Los Angeles, and he lived in the closet of a gym. He had the idea of creating Train To Be Clutch and a top-level boarding school for young kids, but his circumstances were not the best.

He knew enough to know, that if he just listened to his thoughts, those dreams never had a chance. So he began talking to himself using one little phrase: "*I am becoming the leader of a world-changing organization.*"

Even though his circumstances dictated otherwise, Joshua kept saying this out loud. Then, the resistance came and the thoughts hit hard:

> *No, you're not, Joshua! You don't have a degree in sports psychology!*
> "I am becoming the leader of a world-changing organization."

*Joshua, you don't have a real business! You read books and tweet
out quotes!*
"I am becoming the leader of a world-changing organization."

*Joshua, you train three kids who, statistically speaking, probably
won't make it to see their sixteenth birthday!*
"I am becoming the leader of a world-changing organization."

Joshua, you live in a closet and have no money!
"I am becoming the leader of a world-changing organization."

Joshua, you live next to Mr. Clean and a mop!
"I am becoming the leader of a world-changing organization."

Even though his circumstances dictated otherwise, Joshua kept
sowing that belief and vision for himself. The vision was a statement of who he wanted to become as a person so that it allowed
him to have a great impact. Looking back on things now, it's
coming to fruition.

Joshua calls it being "optimistically delusional." I call it courage. It's the easiest thing in the world to go with the opinion
of other people even when you know, deep down, that you
don't believe the same things. It's a courageous act to follow
your heart and do or say what will seem ridiculous to other
people. It takes insane courage to talk to yourself even when
you feel like what you are saying is so far from what you are
currently feeling. But that's the crux of mental toughness. It's
the ability to live according to principles, regardless of your
circumstances.

I still use Joshua's phrase today. I don't know how many times a week I say it, but it's at least sixty times a week that I rattle off that belief statement. It's amazing to see that when I am intentionally talking to myself, I have little capacity to listen to the thoughts floating around in my head.

This concept is not new.

My favorite part of the Bible is the book of Deuteronomy. It's a recollection of the law that God had created for his people, the Israelites. In there, God is preparing them for a period when they will take over a new territory and settle in a fruitful land. The issue, is that the land is currently populated by some of the strongest armies in the world.

God instructs the Israelites to move forward without being deterred by their fears and thoughts about the other armies. His most consistent command to them is *"Remember."*

Remember what I did for you by moving Og, king of Bashan.

Remember what I did to Pharaoh and how he let you leave Egypt.

Do not forget how I provided food that fell from the sky for forty years.

His strongest commandment came to them in the sixth chapter when he told the Israelites to write those events down, talk about them with their kids, and talk about them in the streets with other people.

There is something not only beautiful, but imperative about that command to speak about the events. The more the Israelites actively spoke about the truth of what happened and who God was, the less they focused on the size of the armies and the uncertainty in their circumstances. That's what allowed them to move forward.

It's the same for us. Regardless of what you believe, we need you to speak truth and good fuel into your heart and mind.

Shift Your Focus

It's one thing to acknowledge the thoughts, but it's another thing to focus your attention on something beneficial. If we can identify patterns of thought and the consistent contexts where they arise, we can prepare for them in advance. Let me give you an example.

I know what is likely to happen when I walk in my gym for CrossFit. There is going to be someone in there that I size up and elevate to God-like status. I'm likely to think, *"Oh, he was born for this stuff,"* or *"I could never compete with her."* I know those thoughts aren't helpful or true, but they consistently come up. After those thoughts hit, I can easily settle for a time and weight in my mind that is not scratching my potential.

So here is how I prepare for this in my car or at home before the workout: I acknowledge the likelihood of that thought coming up in the gym. I write the thought down and create an action plan for when it comes up. When it does, I plan to smile. You know, one of those coy smiles like when you are hiding behind the couch and your son takes the bait walking right into your trap and you are about to light him up with foam balls!

After I smile or widen my eyes, I begin to count my reps or count my breaths. Counting is one thing that gets me focused on controllables and rhythm. Lastly, I either say "Choose" out loud with every exhale or I turn to encouraging someone else around me. Literally, I start talking.

It's amazing how this course of action puts me back in a place of clarity and self-control. This is where our best work is accomplished.

If you are not doing something athletic, here is another way it could work.

I know my most repeated thoughts throughout my life have been anxious ones about money and what the future holds. I think many of us would nod along. Let's look at the money thought. Many of us will find ourselves believing that we fit within a certain income bracket. We may not readily admit that, but I know that I did for a long time.

Here is what has helped me.

I know that I will likely think about the need to make more money. If and when that thought comes up, I choose to acknowledge it. I open up my palms towards the sky. I then recite Proverbs 3:1-12. This passage reminds me about who God is and what it looks like to abide in Him. In turn, he tells us what to do with our money.

From there, I turn towards what I can steward that might create more opportunities for me to speak and provide value.

I will be the first to admit I don't always *feel like* turning to these simple steps and, honestly, sometimes I don't pivot. Yet real mental toughness chooses to *grow* in living according to principles, not feelings. It's an ability that you will fail at, but grow in as you continue to move forward.

Remember, greatness isn't for the chosen few. Greatness is for the few who choose to put good fuel into their hearts.

- What are the consistent contexts that elicit some of the most destructive thoughts?
- Construct a phrase that you can intentionally sow using the following prompts:
  - I am becoming _____
  - I am becoming someone who _____
- Commit to sowing these belief statements ten times tomorrow. It may feel wierd, fake, or far from reality. But that's the thing about truth: it's often far from perception.

Vulnerability Is Vital

———

IN ORDER FOR US TO be free, and in order for us to be the best we can in leadership, parenting, and in our sport, vulnerability is vital. Now, vulnerability is not sharing your deepest, darkest secrets with people. Vulnerability is allowing yourself to be fully seen.

I got to speak with Sherri Coale, who coaches the University of Oklahoma women's basketball team, and I asked her a question about vulnerability. She kind of dodged my question, but she gave me an excellent word picture that I don't think I will ever forget. She said, "You know, vulnerability is huge in our program. I tell people all the time that I need your grit."

I said, "What do you mean, 'grit?'" She replied, "Well, you know if it seems like you've got everything together, and things aren't hard for you. If it looks like you don't sweat and you are always perfect and always get done what you want to get done, then you're like a smooth surface. And I can't grab on to you. And I can't go with you."

She continued, "But if you've got some struggles; if I see you striving for excellence and growth; if I see that you sweat and things are hard, and that you fail, and that you have to learn, and that you really have to work at things; then I see that you're like me. You've got some grit, and I can grab on to you. And we can go far together."

Grit, according to Coale, is being real. It's refusing to act like your Instagram highlight reel is your real everyday life. It really comes back down to that scripture in Hebrews 10:14 where it says, "For by one sacrifice Christ has made perfect for all time those who are being perfected."

It really comes down to letting people see the *being perfected* side. It's the *behavior* that is imperfect. The side that's kind of ugly, that doesn't live up to society's standards, that doesn't always make the mark, that doesn't get things right. It's the side that oversleeps and misses scheduled workouts. It's the side that lies when feeling pressure just to make things sound good to those around them. It's the side that does not always use the most loving language. It's the side that jumps to snap judgments. It's the side that really struggles.

It's the side that everyone has. *That's* the side that needs to be available. That's the side that needs to be seen. Or at least, that's the side we need to stop trying to cover up.

It's the grit in our lives that allows us and others to link up and go together.

Vulnerability is vital. Again, vulnerability is *not* sharing your deepest, darkest secrets with people. Vulnerability is allowing yourself to be fully seen.

What we don't need are more people who get on a platform whether at a church, in a boardroom, or on the court and say, "I know I'm not perfect. I have my own struggles, too." I don't care for your cover-all phrase. We also don't need you to flood our inbox or fill every session with a reel of all your faults and failures. We just need you to model progress, not perfection. We need you to give your best energy towards creating rather than covering up. We need to see you striving for progress in the desert. We need you to be open and empathize with us that things are hard. We need you to be real.

Don't Be Fake. Be Real.

One of the "realest" moments I have ever experienced came at a small church gathering in Denver called "Scum Of The Earth." If that name bothers you, it's actually scriptural.[16]

One thing that really bothers me is that too often as believers we try to paint a picture that everything is great. Too often we end up with people who lead worship during services who sound like the theme song from the Lego Movie, "Everything is awesome!"

The guy playing the guitar this particular day got up, strapped on his guitar, and as he was tuning it he just looked at us and said, "We are going to sing *How Sweet It Is To Trust In Jesus.* I am going to drop this into a minor key because if I'm honest, it doesn't always feel sweet to trust in Jesus. And I don't know about you, but I feel pretty shitty right now."

He paused, and everyone felt the depth and reality of that statement. I don't know what was happening in *his* life, but his statement resonated with *my* life.

Then he finished, "But, we know that Jesus is great regardless of how we feel. And that's why we trust Him."

I don't condone cursing to be cool and relevant, but sometimes, some of my most honest prayers involve cursing. I'm not calling God names; I'm trying to adequately describe the depth of my frustration and pain. This gentleman wasn't cursing to be crass or cultural. He used the exact words he felt, and sometimes the word he used is the only word adequate to describe the depth of our pain and despair.

I turned to my wife Amy and we both breathed a sigh of relief. *Finally*, someone got real with us. They said it exactly as it is: God is great, but it doesn't always feel like it. They used the language that we think, but might not say out loud. That day, this gentleman showed his grit, and we linked up and went forward in worship together.

Don't mask the pain. Don't mask the realness of what is going on inside and around you. Don't sweep it under the rug and act like you can hide it. I wonder what would happen if we took all the time, energy, and resources that we use to cover up our grit, and used them to focus on creating solutions and growing? Think about that. How much of your time is consumed by trying to cover your grit?

Don't cover it up and don't sweep it under the rug because when we do, we create a separation between us and the people we lead that says, "I am above reproach. Do as I say."

Well, you are not above reproach. No leader is. I have so many people in leadership who reach out to me and say, "I preach the idea of 1% better all the time to my team." My response is always, "Great! So what are *your* 1% areas *you* are focusing on in *your* life?"

There is always an, "Uuuummmm...well...you know...." And almost always, they don't have the same skin in the game that they are asking of those they lead.

Vulnerability Starts With You

One of the greatest people in leadership I have seen understands vulnerability. She *lives* it.

We did a Skype workshop with the team and I asked everyone, coaches included, to do a controllable intake from the last three weeks. I asked them to write down how much time they gave to the controllables we had talked about and they had agreed to: Time spent reading, reps in visualization, daily "What Went Well" journals, writing out two ways they were going to get better before each practice, writing out controllable keys to success, listening to beneficial audio, etc.

I didn't ask for the results. I just wanted them to see, on paper, what they had been doing with their time. After the workshop the woman coaching called me and said, "Jamie, you crushed me today. I realized I hadn't done *one* of those things in those three weeks. How can I ask my players and coaches to do it if I am not willing to do it too?"

My response to her was to let her team know. Be willing to let them see the scaffolding behind the curtain. Let them see the grit and let them grab onto you. Then move forward setting out your controllable commitments. You probably won't be perfect with those either. But keep moving forward. That's vulnerability in practice - letting people see the imperfect, and the willingness to move forward, anyway. That is courage at its finest.

No one is perfect in their performance or behavior.

Will vulnerability hurt? Absolutely, but like the sweet release of confessing when you have lied to someone close to you, vulnerability disentangles you to operate in your greatness and opens you up to fully connect with others on the journey. When we operate with vulnerability, we have nothing to prove; only value to provide.

- When have you seen vulnerability modeled by someone in a leadership position?
- What is some of the grit that you try to hide from others?
- If others told you that they struggled in those areas, would you think less of them as people?
- What could happen if you took the time, resources, and energy you expend to cover your grit and put that towards providing value or learning and growing?

The Struggle Is Good

"DADDY, I NEED HELP." THIS wasn't really a cry; it was just a calm request from my three year-old son, JJ.

Amy and I were sitting on the sectional in the family room talking while JJ was playing. Our sectional is rounded and backed into a corner, which creates a little nook for JJ to play in. Today was different though.

He usually had a little step stool back there that he used to climb out. I had removed the stool to use in the bathroom, and JJ found himself in a different spot. He didn't have all the tools he was accustomed to using.

So when he asked for help, I replied, "You don't need help, bubba. Just kick your foot off the wall and pull yourself up."

It wasn't that I was lazy. I knew he had the ability to climb out because he is a certified ninja! I saw it as a chance for him to learn how to help himself.

Before even trying, he decided to give up. Turning a little whinier he said, "But daddy, I *can't* do it."

Calmly I just affirmed him and said, "Sure you can, bud. Put one foot on the wall and jump while pulling up on the couch."

He whined some more, asking for help. This went on for about three minutes. As time went on, Amy became more and more uncomfortable. Finally her momma-bear instincts kicked in and it was time to rescue her struggling cub. She set her Bible aside and turned to help him out of the corner.

When she moved to put her Bible aside, JJ began pulling himself up. As she turned, she saw JJ sitting on top of the couch ready to do a flip onto the cushions. Immediately she turned towards me knowing she was about to see my sly grin. "You tried to rescue him from the struggle!" I said in a playful tone. She just looked towards the sky!

It's not that I was being hard on JJ. He moves like a monkey and I knew he could get out. We want to equip JJ to thrive in life. In order for him to learn and prepare, it's imperative that we don't rescue him from the struggle. We do this with discretion allowing him to struggle in things that are not life threatening and in areas that we know he is able to help himself. It's not neglect. It's equipping. The simple truth is, the struggle is usually good for us.

Living off welfare as a single parent became the foothold that J.K. Rowling used to develop her writing skills and create *Harry*

Potter. Steve Jobs said that having to audit classes in college because he couldn't afford them was a launching pad for becoming the leader of some of the greatest companies in the world. The struggle is what allows us to scratch toward our greatest potential.

Think about it athletically. For us to build up strength, we have to meet resistance and struggle with weight and gravity. In order for us to learn how to push through barriers, we need workouts that are mentally taxing. You know, ones where you look at the board and your first impulse is, "There is *no way* I can do that!" All of our workouts don't need to be set up this way, but if none of your workouts scare you, you might not be scratching your potential.

The fact of the matter is: Under pressure, you do not rise to the occasion; you sink to the level of your training. That's a Navy SEAL motto that is worth adopting for yourself.

It's been said that Greek philosophers used to practice speaking with rocks in their mouth so that they developed a deeper understanding of how to speak with an impediment. Patches O'Houlihan, from the movie *Dodgeball*, always reminds me, "If you can dodge a wrench, you can dodge a dodgeball."

I often choose to prepare talks in a noisy household where my son is likely to come in and interrupt me. I welcome the distraction because if I can continue on in my talk while dodging playdough and bouts of screaming, I'll be well able to handle a cell phone ringing or the mic cutting out during one of my talks. Joshua has even had the lights go out at one of his events and he just got louder!

In order to prepare our best, we need to target training in the most callenging environments possible.

Target The Struggle

I heard a great story from Chauncey Billups. Chauncey played in the NBA for years and was one of the best at the point guard position. He told us a story of a time when he got to see Peyton Manning working out.

Chauncey went to the training facility and showed up a little late. Practice was already over and the team had come in from the field. He walked through the facility and into the training room where guys were getting iced and treated. He asked one of the guys in there where Peyton was and the dude said, "He's down the hall. You'll see him."

So Chauncey walked down the hall towards the weight room and started to hear someone yelling. The closer he got the louder the shouting became. When he turned the corner and walked into the weight room, he saw Peyton in the corner on the treadwall. You know, the rock climbing wall that continues to rotate as you climb.

It wasn't really the fact that Peyton was the only one on the team in the weight room after practice that wowed Chauncey. It was what Peyton was doing on top of the workout that wasn't asked of him. Peyton was not only going through the treadwall, but he was shouting out audibles to the possible defenses he was going to face during the season. He was visualizing the defense, communicating as loud as he could, while punishing his body physically. The struggle that he targeted even gave Chauncey the chills!

It's not usually what we do that's asked of us that makes the difference. It's what we chose to do that's not asked of us, while we do what's asked of us, that prepares us to handle what we can't see coming.

But how many of us would choose to avoid that struggle? I did for a very long time!

THE MINDSET NEEDED TO EMBRACE STRUGGLE
Part of my life story was choosing to walk on to a professional soccer team here in Colorado. I was twenty-seven at the time and had been out of soccer for two years with an injury. By the hand of God and some personal courage and risk, I found myself training with the Colorado Rapids. I'll never forget a day in the first week when our coaches said to partner up for one-on-one drills.

I turned to my right and saw Pablo Mastroeni, one of the most decorated players in U.S. soccer history. Internally I said, "Hell, no!!"

I turned to my left and there was a guy named Marvel Wynne who was *the* fastest player in the MLS. "Nope!"

I turned behind me and there was a guy named Andre Akpan, who I heard was an up and coming player. "NOOOO!"

So who did I find? I found this 5'4", 120 lbs, sixteen year-old kid named Bryan who got a hall pass to get out of AP Government to come and train with the Rapids. My justification was that I was going to help this kid learn and grow.

Nonsense! What was I doing? I was trying to take on a challenge, that really wasn't a challenge at all, that I could meet and possibly beat so I could look good. I was trying to fit in for the wrong reasons instead of standing out for the right reasons. I was trying to look like I had it all together so that the guys and coaches would think well of me and I could get a contract.

Come to find out, Bryan was better than me anyways and he made me look like a fool!

I realized that I was living what Carol Dweck calls the "fixed mindset."[17] It's a way of living that keeps us from taking on challenges because we are afraid to fail. It's not so much that the failure sucks, but it's more about the fact that people see our failure and realize that we really aren't *special* or *talented*. Failure becomes something we *are*, instead of something we *do*. If we fail, we often think that we will look weak and won't get on the team, on the floor, or get a promotion.

But what happens when you are willing to fail consistently while also taking in valuable information? I mean you actually use the mistakes instead of letting the mistakes use you. If you do that long enough, something good will happen. It did for me.

I began to take on the best players in practice when I could. I was getting beat 14-1, but something changed. It wasn't about the result. I wasn't walking away saying, "I got beat 14-1, so today I was a failure."

Success for me was redefined: *"What did I learn today that will make me better?"* I was studying the guys I got to go up against. I was watching their hips and eyes and seeing what made them successful. The more I studied them, the more I applied what made them successful. I did this for eight weeks and the results started to get better.

One day we were doing one-on-one drills as a team and I saw the other team all shuffling in line. One of the guys on my team came up to me and said, "Jamie, do you know what they are all doing over there? No one wants to go against you because you are killing them in this drill!"

Now, you could ask any guy on the team and they would probably tell you that I wasn't a threat to their playing time. But in that tiny piece of soccer, one-on-one, on that day, I was crushing it!

I didn't get a contract with the team, but it never really was about the contract. You may never get the promotion, but it's not about the promotion. You may never see the court, but it's not about *this* season. It's about who we become. That time at the Rapids was less about getting a $34,000 contract for the year; it was a context or training-ground for who I was becoming as a dad, husband, mentor and follower of Christ. What I learned and developed in that time has radically altered the trajectory of my life.

Embracing the "growth mindset," in which anything that happens is in your best interest, is a scary thing to do. Standing out for the right reasons instead of fitting in for the wrong reasons is not going to make you popular or feel good. It's not a short-term strategy. It's not a *Do-this-once-and-you'll-be-good* strategy. It's a long-term lifestyle. It's also one that will alter the trajectory of your life, your organization's culture, and your family's legacy for generations to come.

It's a simple principle: if you skip the struggle, you skip your greatness.

- What struggles did you choose not to skip that you are grateful for now?
- Where have you found yourself intentionally avoiding struggle?
- Where is the fixed mindset popping up in your life?
- In what areas of your life can you start to target struggle?

Up Until Now

———

I LIKE TO START OFF my workshops with a little activity. Imagine yourself in the crowd and follow my instructions.

Turn towards a partner and both of you stick out your right hands towards one another. Have your hand open with your thumb pointing towards the sky.

Now clasp your other four fingers together with your partner. And on the count of three, try to get your partner's thumb down.

One, two, three, go!

If you were in the crowd what would you do?

If you are like 95% of the people in my workshops, you will start thumb wrestling. Some of you will go back into third grade and really get in to it. Some of you are feeling great because you're really good at thumb wars. Others of you aren't thrilled because you've never won a thumb war before.

But who said anything about thumb wrestling?

The instructions were very simple: try to get your partner's thumb down. And just about everyone turns it into a win-lose proposition. Very few, maybe one percent of thousands actually make it a win-win. You could say to your partner, "I'll let you get my thumb down with your right hand and I'll get your's down with my left."

Why do we turn to a win-lose model? Because that's what we have always done in that position. When else do you get in a thumb war position with your hands?

What we tend to do is get in situations and draw on past experiences to piece together all the rules or ideas about how one moves forward, and then we act accordingly. Or, like the four percent in the workshops, we wait a few seconds while watching everyone else, and when their actions confirm our initial thoughts, we feel assured and act accordingly.

One of the greatest inhibitors to your personal greatness is that you are likely living according to the patterns you have seen in the past.

We all see patterns. Like the woman playing golf who made bogey on 16, 17, and 18 in *every* round of golf for the last three years of her life.

Like me seeing my lack of follow up with clients and organizations that I get to work with.

Like the woman in coaching who said she tried giving autonomy to her team for three weeks and saw no visible return on the investment.

Or like the gentleman I know who says he can never see himself according to his worth rather than performance, because that's the way it's always been.

We all see patterns and often it's the patterns we've seen that we bring about in the present.

The patterns are not set in stone. They are simply ruts that we have carved out in the dirt by repetitive ways of thinking and consistent choices. You don't have to follow the rut, but it's difficult at first to carve a new path.

Let's take the woman who consistently bogeyed the last three holes. She was terribly frustrated and dejected, but when she told me what was happening I just smiled. Why? Because that was in the past.

"You're right," I said, "That stuff has happened. And *up until now*, you, by your own admission, have played out of fear, trained minimal hours, been very unfocused in your practice, have had less than beneficial self-talk, negatively visualized, and have compared yourself to everyone around you."

"*Up until now*, that is how you have operated, and the results have been similar. But everything changes when we *consistently* change our now."

I've undergone this one in a physical fitness sense. When I started to train hard to play professionally again, things were terrible. The weight that I was moving, the times I was running and the length of time it took for me to recover were at a very low level. So, I asked myself this question:

Jamie, if you consistently work with your trainer, alter your sleeping habits, consistently use world-class recovery techniques, change your diet to that of an Olympian, and begin to work on competing vs. comparing, and do all of that for six months, do you think that your times will stay the same?

The answer is obviously, "NO!" Even if I only consistently worked on three of those areas, which I did for the first three months, I should not expect the same results. Why? Because I have changed my *now*.

Your *now* might be:

- Going for a walk four days a week
- Choosing to write five things you are grateful for when you drink your coffee
- Working on competing vs. comparing with others
- Writing out a cue card detailing how you want to respond in various situations
- Listening to "Beneficial Beliefs" audio
- Doing consistent "What Went Well" journals
- Using purposeful visualization
- Holding to a strict nutritional plan
- Reading good content

And the list could go on.

What if you started working on one or two of these things consistently? Should you expect the same results? No. But could you get the same results? Absolutely! If we live in the old way of thinking and follow those ruts, it undercuts and often nullifies all the work we put in.

Do It Long Enough For It To Make A Difference

A woman who plays golf spoke with me about a few things she felt were holding her back. Two of the things were inconsistency with her swing and handling emotions. Because of a few other things she mentioned, we started working on developing a pre-shot routine. I wanted her to develop a routine that she could train and trust so that she didn't slow down or speed up before shots.

I asked her if she had a routine already and she said, "I've never found one that stuck."

My reply was, "Have you not found one that's stuck or have you not stuck with one long enough for it to actually make a difference?"

She wasn't happy with that question because we both knew the answer.

So we created a routine that I wanted her to practice on every shot both in practice and in rounds. I said, "I want you to stick to this every shot for two weeks."

Immediately, her body started tensing up and there was a look of *"There is no way I can do that!"* written all over her face.

"Are you uncomfortable with that?" I asked.

"I've never done that before," she confided. "I don't think I've stuck with anything in life for that long!"

That's simply not true. That's just how we've interpreted the pattern. As we unpacked it she's been very consistent with brushing her teeth, eating, shopping, and verbally beating the hell out of herself.

But the crux of the matter is if she changes her *now*, we should never expect the same results.

I'm not encouraging people to think about expectations and visualize results. What I am encouraging is that we first start to change what we do now and then we start to believe that what we are doing will produce different results and break the patterns that we have seen in the past. But we have to do it long enough for it to actually make a difference.

Principles Into Practice
What are three things you could commit to consistently working on for the next three weeks? Be very specific, and I'd encourage you to think small.

Have you ever operated like this? If the answer is no, then you have no idea how things could change in the future. You need to believe that your mode of operation and results will not be the same in the future.

Here is a phrase that you will use:

Up   until   now   _____.   BUT   NOW, _____.

For me, up until the last year, I had lived out of fear and a scarcity mindset. BUT NOW, I choose to operate out of love and abundance. This has created 'new normals' in my life, my business, and for my family.

What could your 'BUT NOW' statements be? Create five for yourself.

Here are some examples from a friend who coaches at the Division 1 level, and is working hard to become transformational.

Up until now, I have worried about what others think of me in coaching and parenting. ***BUT NOW***, I make decisions out of love and with conviction.

Up until now, when I walk into a room I have been fearful of how others are judging me. ***BUT NOW***, I choose to remember that I am no longer judged and am free to love others.

Up until now, I have worried about sounding dumb and whether or not someone wants to talk to me on the phone. ***BUT NOW***, I choose to ask questions to understand, and share stories where appropriate.

Up until now, I have tried to please everyone in my decisions so that I don't hurt feelings. ***BUT NOW,*** I make decisions drawing on wisdom and believing that the decisions are in everyone's best interest.

Up until now, I have felt bad delegating tasks to other people. ***BUT NOW,*** I choose to utilize the gifts that those around me have while respecting their boundaries.

Up until now, I have worried about saying hard things to help people move forward. ***BUT NOW,*** I choose to touch on real issues because I love them too much to let them stay where they are.

Up until now, I have worried that I ask God for too much. ***BUT NOW*** I choose to engage with my Father as often as I can.

Up until now, I have been waiting for the wheels to come off of anything that is going well. ***BUT NOW*** I choose to enjoy and focus on being at my best in the present, knowing I cannot control the future.

Up until now, my team's mistakes have consumed my energy and focus. ***BUT NOW*** I choose to see the things that they are doing well and fan those into flames.

Up until now, I have been afraid of failing and have chosen to play it safe. ***BUT NOW*** I choose to take on tough challenges that put me outside my comfort zone.

Up until now, I have had no boundaries and some in my family have suffered as I devoted attention to my team, business, and certain individuals. ***BUT NOW*** I am giving my best to those I love and decisively say no to things outside of my core commitments and mission for my life.

Up until now, I have not been very prayerful and have not devoted my life entirely to Christ. ***BUT NOW*** I choose to trust in Him and lean not on my own understanding.

These are not easy or comfortable changes. Just saying these phrases doesn't change everything. These have to be coupled by tangible action. Sowing these beliefs and coupling them with action is a step of great faith. And guess what? There will be failure in every single category. But they at least get us started sowing beneficial fuel into our hearts instead of repetitively living in the patterns that we have seen in the past.

As I write the final draft of this book, I have just returned from visiting my friend and her team. During the last practice, my friend walked in with a young girl who they were recruiting. Her assistant coach leaned toward me and said, "A year ago she would never have spent time with a recruit one-on-one. She always felt she would sound stupid."

Scroll up a little bit in this chapter and read the third belief statement she made and sowed. Much has changed by a suttle yet profound shift in her language.

It takes courage to step out and work on changing patterns. But it's exactly what we are asking of those we parent, lead and coach. We want them to do what they haven't done so that they can become who they have never been. We want them to try what they have never tried so that they can go where they have never gone.

All of this requires faith. Dr. Martin Luther King Jr. said, "Faith is taking a step when you cannot see the entire staircase." And honestly, that's how it feels.

If we want new patterns for those we influence, let's live a life of creating new patterns ourselves.

- In what ways have you always reacted in certain contexts?
- How would you like to respond instead?
- What are some beliefs you've had about yourself in the past that you want to begin letting go of?

What Is Greater Than *Why*

———

THE NUMBER ONE QUESTION WE *want* to ask is usually the worst question we *can* ask. It's the source of almost all pain, and it usually causes people to self-shame. How often do you ask it? To whom do you ask it?

The question is "Why?"

I get it. In coaching young kids or older kids, we want to ask them, "Why did you pass it to Sarah instead of taking the shot yourself?" Really what we are thinking is, *The choice you just made wasn't the most optimal decision and you probably should have done something else. But I'm going to try and lead you to figuring it out yourself* (and this is usually done with palms up, shoulders shrugged, and a look of "WTF" written all over our face)."

I want them to figure it out themselves too, but *why* is not the pathway.

When someone asks you, *"Why* did you wear that shirt today?" are you most likely to stay calm or get defensive?

What about when your assistant coach asks, "*Why* did you start John instead of Mark?"

What about when your boss asks you *why* you submitted a slightly different proposal to the client you are working with?

What about when your coach asks you *why* you chose to hit that club?

Most of us have experienced "*Why?*" as a question that is dripping with judgment. That's the bias we carry when we hear it. My father-in-law can ask me why I made the coffee with hazelnut and immediately I will feel like he is angry with me.

I, like most of us, have experienced *why* as a way of shame and therefore it puts me in a place where I want to lash out and say "Who the _____ are you to question my choice in coffee beans?!?" or it puts me in a place of shame where I say, "I'm sorry! Do you not like it? I'll never do it again. Jamie, you are an idiot!"

Questions Equip For Life
What's worse is that we equip people through the questions we ask them. The questions we consistently ask to those whom we influence are questions they learn to ask themselves. Our language matters!

I was asked *why* a lot growing up in different capacities. I learned that *why* must be the pathway to greater understanding and growth. Here's what happened to me.

I made a mistake.

Joshua and I were living in Boulder, Colorado playing with a developmental team during the summer of our sophomore year at Vanderbilt. One day we went out to the local department store and I did something ridiculous. I grabbed a pair of fake $9.99 diamond stud earrings.

No, they weren't for Amy. They were for me!

I put them in my pocket and tried to leave without paying for them. When we got to the door I was confronted by a guy yelling at me, "Give me the earrings!!!" Joshua and I ended up in handcuffs, were threatened with charges being pressed against us, and sat in a little interrogation room for a few hours. By the way, Joshua had nothing to do with this!

I ended up having to pay a $200 fine, but worse than the fine was the self-shame that lasted for months. I asked myself, "Jamie, *why* did you do that?"

Which was really more like *Jamie, only a* _____
_____ *idiot would do such a dumb*
_____ *thing like that* (enter any expletive you want!)*!!*

That's how I had been asked that question, and that's what I said to myself. The only answer I could consistently find for *why* I did it was "I'm a _____ing idiot and a horrible person."

But that's not completely true. If we use *why* to self-shame, we usually complete a caricature of how horrible we are. We are not confronted with the evidence of how kind, considerate, driven, loving, and friendly we are. We don't think about the lack of thievery in our past.

We only turn to the bad stuff, and we usually blow it out of proportion. We call ourselves the vilest of names that we would hesitate to repeat to anyone else. If you're like me, there's the danger that the thoughts then slip to how your best friend would never make such a dumb mistake. Now you're in comparison, and that's an even worse place!

It all starts with what most experts in the world will say you need to know: *Why?*

A Better Question

There is a better question than *why*. The question is "What?"

"What did you do?"

Follow it up with *"If you could do it again, would you do it differently? How so?"*

When we ask people *what* they did, they can give us an answer according to objective evidence: I stole the earrings. When we ask people *why* they did it, they often can't explain it, or they will sometimes create a *why* that sounds good. We are awfully good at justifying what we do!

I remember living in Ireland on a small budget and deciding to get the bigger cable package for the TV. My justification to Amy was that *then* I could have the guys on the team over to watch football and get to know them better. Nonsense! In three years I had one person over! I just made my *why* compelling enough so that I could get what I wanted.

Why is destructive. *What* is restorative. Asking *what* they did is not usually leading people to a place of shame, and when we are asking ourselves how we would do it differently, we are really leading ourselves to the growth mindset. We are heading towards understanding that we are not our past, we are not our performance, and we are not our potential. But everything is an opportunity to learn and grow.

We lead others down the line of actually learning from the experience so they can make great choices instead of creating a culture of fear where they don't want to mess up again. The fear of failure is killing our teams, strangling our organizations, tearing apart our families, and restricting people from tapping their true greatness.

Shame doesn't equip; it strangles. And we contribute to that fear-culture every time we ask *why*.

- When has *Why?* led you down the path of shame and defeat?
- When do you consistently use *Why?* or hear it said in contexts around you?
- I wonder what will change for you and others as you start to shift and maybe forty percent of the time ask *What?* instead.

- PRINCIPLE 18 -

The Obstacle Is The Way

———

BOB GOFF IS ONE OF my favorite people and I've never met him. But his book has radically affected me. What I love about Bob is that there seems to be nothing that shuts him down and keeps him from moving forward with his life and his mission. I'm not saying he doesn't struggle, but I know he doesn't stop.

When Bob wanted to get into law school, he was told that his scores were not good enough. Most of us would get that letter from admissions and take it as an authoritative stamp that we cannot proceed with our dream. But Bob is a solutions guy. Well, really he's more about just being passionately curious and ridiculous, but he always seems to find a solution.

Bob made a choice. Not the choice many of us *would* make. But a choice that all of us *could* make. He decided to sit outside of the dean's office until he let him into the school.

Every time the dean came out of his office Bob would say, "I know you can tell me to go get my books." The dean would walk by him a few times a day and Bob would say the same thing over and over.

I'm sure the dean's amusement turned into annoyance as his schedule was disrupted. I know he had to start going to the bathroom less!

But Bob stuck to his plan, even as the semester started. While all the students who were invited into the school went to classes, Bob stayed in his process. He knew there was a way. Finally, the door opened. "Go get your books."

Where many of us would see an obstacle, Bob saw an opportunity, and he got what he desired. But with any obstacle, it's not *just* the opportunity to get something we want, it's the opportunity to become someone greater.

Sure Bob got what he wanted, and in the process of challenging the obstacles, Bob became someone who wouldn't stop at *NO*. Who he became in that context prepared him for greater challenges down the road - like making it illegal for witchdoctors in Uganda to sacrifice young children.

You don't accomplish something like that by just graduating from law school. You do that because of who you've chosen to become. Many people have degrees from institutions, but they don't have the resolve to challenge the status quo. It's in challenging the obstacles that we sharpen our character. When push comes to shove, we won't rise to the occasion; we will sink to the level of our training and the depth of our character.

GO *THROUGH* THE MOUNTAIN OR GO *AROUND* IT?

TJ loved basketball growing up. He was encouraged by his dad to try football and baseball, but TJ followed his passion. He was kind of stocky and short, and really didn't seem like he would excel in his sport of choice.

Regardless, TJ tried out for two local AAU teams, and they both cut him. Now, TJ could have tried to "Bob Goff" the teams. Maybe he could serve as an assistant on the team and train on the side. That's an option in the face of the obstacle, but there are plenty of other viable solutions.

TJ did what most of us would not probably do at fifteen. He started his own AAU team. Like a real legit AAU team.

He started the team.

He raised the money.

He hired a coach.

He found a gym for rent.

How did he raise the money? Simple, according to him. Have each kid write a bio, and create a program. Then sell half-page ads to local businesses for $25 and full-page ads for $50.

The way he says it, it's as much of a no brainer as, *"You just brush your teeth every day."*

TJ didn't come from a family of wealth. He didn't have endless resources at hand. No matter, he had been preparing for this moment for years. He was being mentored by a young guy who had helped him with his basketball game, who started his own small company out of college. Every summer in high school he had TJ cold-calling hundreds of people a day. "It taught me a lot" he said, "I knew I had to get through 99 no's to get to the one yes."

He went on to say that his mentor had him reading books from Dale Carnegie and other stories of people overcoming odds, and he realized what was possible with grit and persistence.

So, instead of going through the obstacle, TJ went around it. He didn't avoid it and turn around. He still made progress, but in a less obvious way. The only way TJ lives that story is by developing the character to meet challenges with creativity and passion. And it's his ability to meet those challenges that allows him to be effective in his coaching at the college level.

I wonder what kind of creative solutions you could start to find if you spent less time looking at the mountain, and more time accruing and applying wisdom? I wonder what will change as you move from a posture of "the problem is" to "the possibility is?"

PIVOT AND ADAPT

I thought he was joking. But his facial expression was different than I've seen before. He legitimately looked scared and embarrassed. "I don't have the keys," Joshua told me as we arrived at the car.

As I laid my snowboard down and took off all my gear, Joshua kept unzipping and zipping his thirteen pockets on his jacket. It finally hit me; he was serious.

We were in Vail, Colorado and had just finished two days of snowboarding and talking about the new year as a company. I was hesitant to join him on this trip because Amy was due with our little girl in the next week. But she literally forced me, and one of my principles is "Do not cross a pregnant mama bear!"

Thinking about the options in the parking garage didn't get either of us excited. For Joshua, the rental car company would have to tow a new car two hours up from Denver, break into our current rental, and tow it back. The dollar signs started spinning: Fee for new car, lost key replacement, rebooking Joshua's flight home, getting a hotel, food, etc.

For me, I knew I wouldn't be home until the early morning the next day, and anything could happen with Amy, our son JJ, and the little peanut to come.

As we sat at the lodge for a few hours, Joshua was on the phone with a friend sharing the situation and she was pissed: "You're having the worst day possible and you are probably going to write about it, and it's probably going to make you a lot of money! You suck!"

She was right. Not about the fact that *this* story would make him (or me) money, but that the story of obstacles would. Why? Because our encounters with obstacles are just that: stories. And it's the stories we live, not just the ones we tell, that can change the lives of those around us.

The new rental car showed up around eleven at night. As we left Vail Village, I said, "If nothing else, in this whole venture with Train To Be Clutch, we've become highly adaptable people."

And that's the crux of mental training. How adaptable are we? Are we choosing to develop that characteristic in our lives, our families, and our teams? Because obstacles are going to come. But it's our ability to pivot, adapt, and move forward in spite of those circumstances that really matters.

There is always a way forward. Sometimes it's going around. Sometimes it's going over. Sometimes it's just walking straight forward and watching the obstacle move. But what I care about for you is that you become a person who sees opportunity where most others see obstacles. I care that you seek solutions in the midst of setbacks, that your creative genius kicks in when your circumstances cave in.

There is always a solution to be found. There is always a back door. That said, it's not so much that we need to find them. We simply need to become people who are *set* on finding them, regardless of how we feel.

You want to write your book, but you have to work your current job? Great! Writing your book while in your job might actually produce a more passionate style in your writing. You can write about real issues in the moment of actually experiencing them. Your obstacle is the way forward.

If you don't feel like you have the time, then adapt. I wrote the majority of the bones for this and three other books on my phone using a dictation app. I recorded snapshots of thoughts and conversations on my phone while driving, walking, and, I'm sorry but, while in the bathroom. Your obstacle of not having big chunks of time is actually the thing that will allow you to push past resistance a little bit easier.

Without a doubt, the number one obstacle people say they face is themselves. Guess what? You are also the way forward. Most of us don't have a capital or cash problem, we just aren't set on finding creative solutions and doing the neccessry work to move closer to our dreams.

Nothing serves as a better teacher than going through difficult seasons and experiences. If we're honest, we *feel* like skipping the struggle and difficulty, but it's the struggle that equips and connects.

- What are some obstacles that you consistently face? What are they keeping you from doing or becoming?
- What's been your typical response when you face those obstacles?
- What are some creative solutions on how to lean in to those pieces of resistance? You need to look outside of what is being done by everyone else and try to find solutions that work for you.

- PRINCIPLE 19 -

First Things First

———

I LOVE MY WIFE FOR many reasons. Up there on the list is that she usually doesn't do the dishes. It's not because she sucks at it, but because it's really not that important.

I put in a lot of hours and I come home at the end of my workday and there's absolute chaos. We've got a three-month-old crying. We've got a three-year-old throwing Paw Patrols around the house. I'm tired from two workouts and six hours of work. We've got my father-in-law telling us all sorts of things about the yard and how it's not growing and the rabbits are eating the grass. To top it off, the kitchen is absolutely obliterated. I'm the one who cooks and I have to clean the dishes *before* I can cook.

And I love it. Do you know why?

Because a dirty kitchen is usually the evidence that Amy put first things first that day. I care more about her interactions with our children. I care more about Amy taking time to read scripture and read things that are important to her. I care more about her spending time with people who she wants to spend time with. In comparison, I care little about how the kitchen looks.

I know there are many of you who say you wouldn't be able to operate your best knowing that the kitchen is a mess. You're probably right. It's a struggle for Amy and I too, because for a long time we were conditioned to care more about how it looks, than what it actually is. But real leadership is not about getting things done. Real leadership is about living a mission that others can follow.

AN OBSESSION WITH HOW IT LOOKS

When I talk with people who coach golf, they all agree that most players care more about how their swing *looks*, than what it actually does. I see this in plenty of colleges during their recruiting process. They care more about how the facilities look and seem rather than actually engaging in a deep process of mentoring and connection. What they create long-term is an environment that is based on how things look, rather than what they are.

I remember a moment in college when a friend came for his official visit to Vanderbilt. I had played with this guy for nine years and I was pumped that he was thinking of joining the team. I remember walking the campus with him after we had just finished playing a small-sided game in the racquet-ball courts. I asked him what he thought of everything and his answer shocked me. He thought it was nice, but another school he visited had better equipment. They had an underwater treadmill.

I was dumbfounded! I was waiting for him to laugh, but he was dead serious! Was he planning on being injured the majority of his career? That's what those treadmills are for!

He ended up going to that school - maybe for the treadmill, and maybe for other reasons. But that story has always stood out in my mind when I think about first things first. If we care more about what it looks like than what it actually does or is, *we* are the ones who miss out in the long run.

RESPONSIBLY IRRESPONSIBLE

Putting first things first usually means that it looks irresponsible and ugly to other people.

I remember Gary Vaynerchuk, who runs VanyerMedia, talking about how he spends his time. On the video he unpacks how the majority of his day is spent going on people's twitter profiles, seeing what they talk about, seeing how they interact, and actually interacting with them. He spends much of the day scrolling on his phone so that he understands the ins and outs of what really engages people on social media and what really moves the needle for companies.

During the video he stops and shows his email inbox. There was an email from an important client who pays him loads of money for his services, yet Gary hadn't responded to the email from five days ago. Why? That client pays him because he is *the* world's leading expert on social media. The reason he works with that company is because he does the dirty hard work of putting first things first, and it doesn't look right to everyone else. He's not doing it out of laziness or carelessness. He is modeling what his client and company need to live to be influential.

You need to do the same. What kind of things do you attend to that are not first things, but are things that are only about looking good to others?

Second Things Put First

I was at a professional golf event recently with Kevin. Kevin went in the clubhouse to grab something to eat while I was standing outside next to his bag responding to emails. As he walked out of the clubhouse there was an elderly lady who was about to walk in. Instead of holding the massive oak door for her, he let it close on her arm. Kevin just kept walking right towards the bag and I. He pulled out his phone, checked the time, then scooped up the bag and started walking towards the practice green.

I couldn't believe what I saw!

A few days later Kevin was asking me what I saw on the weekend that we could be working on. "Kevin, I want to tell you this in love. But you acted like an ass during the tournament. I don't believe that you are an ass, but you acted like one."

I told him what happened with the elderly lady and we both started laughing. Not because it's cool to slam the door on a lady. But because of how ridiculous the situation was.

He tried to justify it, "Was it the day of the first round, because I get into a deep zone on those days."

No Kevin, it was the day of the pro-am, but even if it was the day of the first round, that still doesn't justify what you did.

Again, Kevin isn't an ass. He had just fallen prey to what we all face: the alluring rhythm of putting second things first. Being so caught up in what we *feel like* is important, that we miss out on what *actually is* important. I don't care what level of sport you play; your performance in that sport is not really what matters most. It's who you are becoming and the effect you have on others.

People should not be seen as impediments to the success of your career. They are people. Acknowledge them. Your career will only go as far and wide as the depth of your character.

The funny thing is that when Kevin keeps his priorities straight and actually notices and engages with people and treats them like human beings, his golf is a secondary thing. Subsequently he plays more freely. When he plays in freedom, he scores pretty low on the course. When you put those first things first, the secondary things are not suppressed. They actually *increase.*

Scarcity And Lack

While I was in Ireland playing soccer I developed a pretty serious injury to my pelvis. The pain was so excruciating that it hurt to walk, cough, and just sit up in bed. The doctor told me I had an injury to the pelvis that many women get after delivering their children. Cheers, doc!

The protocol for recovery was to keep from running and kicking and to do small movements that would strengthen my pelvic floor. These workouts felt like ridiculousness compared to the amount of energy and grit that went into our practices. And if I'm honest, it frustrated the hell out of me.

Usually, the first things we need to put first are often the things that are so seemingly miniscule that we skip over them. They are easy to do and easy *not* to do. You won't notice their benefits after only a few times of doing them.

My team was having an up and down season during my recovery and I desperately wanted to play. So I bought a belt that was supposed to hold my pelvis secure and started playing again only after a few weeks. What I thought was a noble and captain-like move, turned out to be an eighteen-month delay in recovery. I made the issue worse and sat out for the better part of two years.

My desire to accelerate the process actually impeded the process. It was my feeling of not having enough time that made me try to speed things up. In the same way, it's usually our feelings of scarcity or lack that cause us to skip the first things.

Whether it's taking time to properly recover, sending a text to our spouse that we will be home late, making time to engage in a *meaningful* conversation with someone in our organization, sending a video tweet or email saying thank you, or letting the garlic and onions sizzle long enough in the pan before you start cooking the meat, it's imperative that we acknowledge the second things, set them aside, and first do the essentials very *very* well.

Oh, I get it. There are emergencies. There are moments where something most pressing can require our attention. But if we're honest, most of what we claim to be an "emergency" or *of most importance* is actually laughable when you see it on paper.

As Greg McKeown reminds me, "We cannot underestimate the unimportance of just about everything."[18] Honestly, there are very few things that matter in the world. We don't need a near-death experience to know that. We just need to acknowledge our tendencies in certain contexts to put second things first, and choose to write a new story.

- Make a list of the first things in your life.
- What are the second things that you tend to put before the first things?
- If you put the first things first, what is the immediate issue that arises in your mind?
- If the first things are put first for the next three months, what do you think will happen to your overall results?

Everything Matters. Everyone Matters.

––––––

A FRIEND OF MINE COACHES basketball at a D-1 school. He called me one day while I was at Golfsmith to tell me that he was offered a new job. The school pursuing him is a household name from a power conference. They had offered him a lot of money and some pretty amazing perks.

"I can't believe that out of the whole country they want me! I mean, I have one year of head coaching experience and our record last season was 14-18."

We unpacked things a little further and I asked a question: Would taking the job undercut any of your deepest held principles?

He was quiet for a moment and then said, "I've always told kids and parents that I am in this for the long haul. I'm not going to be one of those coaches who ups and leaves for more money at a big name school."

Sounds like a principle to me! He acted in line with his principle. He turned the job down twice, even after he was offered more money.

As we talked further I asked him how this all came about. He said that his team had lost to the powerhouse last season. The coach was resigning and when asked who would be a good fit, he mentioned my friend. Though he had lost the game, the way my friend treated the opposing coach, opposing players, his own staff and own players was above reproach.

My friend concluded, "I always thought that my progress in the coaching ranks was dependent on my wins and losses. But I have realized it's more about my character."

My friend didn't know it at the time when they lost, but everything he was doing mattered. He didn't take the job, but who he became was at least one of the important variables in their success on and off the court this past season. As they made a run to a conference championship and a dance at the NCAA tournament, it was clear: everything matters.

Everyone Matters

A number of years ago an elderly couple wandered into a small hotel in downtown Philadelphia. It was 1:00 A.M., pouring down rain and they desperately needed a room. The young clerk said there were no rooms available and, even worse, there was a convention in town and there wasn't a room in the entire city.

"But I can't send you away," he said. "I have a staff room here in the back that you can sleep in. You can shower and rest up and stay warm." The couple resisted, not wanting to be a burden, but the young clerk insisted they stay. So they showered, slept, and in the morning they thanked him for his kindness.

"You ought to be the manager of the finest hotel in the world!" the older man said. Then they packed up the car and went on their way.

About two years later the young clerk received a letter from a name unfamiliar to him. Inside was an invitation to visit New York and round-trip ticket. So he packed up his bags and went. A driver collected him from the airport and took him downtown where a brand new building was rising into the sky. He got out of the car and the elderly man from that night two years ago stuck his hand out to introduce himself.

"In case you don't remember me, my name is William Waldorf Astor and this is our very first Waldorf Astoria Hotel. William Bolt, I want you to be its manager."

I love this story and I know you may have already read it. We included it in *Burn Your Goals* and I followed it with this question:

What would it look like if we treated every person, client, and opportunity as if it was our dream opportunity?

The question sounded good, but it's a *terrible* question. It's evidence of where my heart was at the time. People are not *opportunities*. People are people.

Everyone matters because each and every person is a human being. Every interaction matters, because they're refining who we are becoming.

TREAT PEOPLE LIKE PEOPLE

I was just on the other side of one of the most emotional moments in my life. Vanderbilt had cut their men's soccer team two days before our spring semester started. When I heard the news, I burst out of the locker room in tears and ran to our unlit stadium and bawled me eyes out like someone had died.

I tried calling my mom, but she didn't answer. I called my dad and like a little toddler sobbed out, "Dad they cut the program!" I remember the calm and conviction in his voice, "Ok," he reassuringly said. "We'll pray about it and figure out the next move."

Much happened over the next two days, which landed me in a new city. I transferred to study and play at the University of Memphis and knew absolutely no one. I was sleeping on a cot in my new teammates' laundry room while trying to actually get enrolled in classes. While lying there one night, I remember reflecting on a question: "Without soccer, who am I?"

I had faced this question a few days ago and realized my identity had been completely wrapped up in soccer and how I performed. I was tired of the emotional roller coaster that ensued, and began to wonder *who* I wanted to be. Afterall, no one at this school knew me. I knew that the way I interacted with the team during the first week would determine what values people knew I wanted to live by. But I didn't think about the values. I thought about a person.

If I could be like anyone, I want to be like Tim Lonergan.

Tim was a teammate of mine at Vanderbilt and a good friend. He was a better friend to me than I was to him if I'm honest. We came in the same year, at the same position, and I had the lion's share of minutes on the field. Tim was a great player, but he was an even better person.

Even though I was beating him out for playing time, he would stay behind and share things he could see from the bench that I could do to improve my play. I couldn't believe how he treated me! If the roles had been reversed, I would have been very bitter. But not Tim. Even though he is one of the fiercest competitors I've ever met, his compassion and love for people was something that seemed to be without conditions.

Tim was a follower of Christ, and everyone knew it. Not because he preached to us, but because he lived such a loving life. At the time I *said* I was a follower of Jesus, but my life was far from it. Yet Tim never pushed and never pointed fingers. He always had his hand out, palm open, excited for me to join him no matter what we were doing.

As I lay there on the cot, memory after memory started to fill my mind of Tim's love for me and the courage he showed in standing up for what he believed. It hit me: I wanted to be like Tim.

It wasn't long after that I began reading the Bible and joining other believers. I started that semester off declining to drink while at the team party, and so went the rest of the year.

I don't know any other person who has had such a profound impact on me in such a short period of time. It wasn't any single event that made me want to be like Tim. It wasn't anything that he particularly said. It was how he consistently operated in just about every interaction for two and a half years. He didn't know it at the time, but he probably saved my life and, without question, he has radically altered the trajectory of our family for generations to come.

I don't know what you are going through right now. I don't know what kind of menial tasks you have lined up for today. I have no idea how things are going to pan out for you. But I do know that you have amazing opportunities all around you. They may not be tasks that others will see or that will make a sudden change to your situation, but how you choose to operate in the moment is altering who you become and how you will consistently execute in the future.

- Who has had a Tim-like impact on your life?
- What is it about them that impacted you so deeply?
  - Take a minute to relive one of those specific instances right now.
- What do people get when they consistently get you?

It's Just A Signal

———

A FRIEND AND CLIENT OF mine excitedly called to tell me about one of his greatest struggles in the week. Because he plays a professional sport, I imagined it had something to do with the latest competition. I was wrong.

He said, "I went out to get some sushi on the road this week. I sat down and ordered my usual four rolls. When it finally came out, I was so ready to eat it, but I couldn't because she brought me chopsticks."

"Ok," I said. "So what's the problem with chopsticks?"

"I don't know how to use them. But I didn't want to call the waitress back over and ask for a fork because then she would be like, *'Who is this clown that doesn't know how to use chopsticks? What, are you five years old?'*"

"So what did you do?" I asked.

"I just sat there for a few minutes looking at my food! And then it hit me that if I tried to use the chopsticks, then I would end up with sushi all down my shirt anyways and I'd for sure look like a fool then."

"So what happened next?" I inquired.

"I called the lady over and asked if she could bring me a fork. So she did. "

"And then what happened?" I prodded.

"She just walked away to the next table. She didn't say anything! She didn't even care!"

Now, we can sit there and point at my friend and laugh, but really I don't think his bout with fear is too dissimilar to what many of us are getting hung up on. Whether it's the fear of failure, the fear of looking dumb, the fear of what others think, or the fear of missing out, fear is fear, and we need to learn how to use it instead of letting it use us.

Real quick, though: Think about one of the fears that you have that is holding you back in a certain area or context in your life. It could be the fear of not getting recruited, making an error in a game, being rejected by a significant other, losing your job, speaking publicly, praying with your spouse, addressing an issue that might cause conflict, saying "Sorry," writing a book, quitting your job, telling a client "No," or fear about what the future holds.

These are all legitimate fears, just like my friend had. The presence of fear does not mean that you are weak. It doesn't mean there is anything wrong with you. *Everyone* experiences it. Some of the people who are the best in the world at what they do admit to *constantly* having the presence of fear. But they learn to use it, instead of letting it use them. Significant things will change in your life and organization when you learn how to retrain the signal.

A SIGNAL VS A VERDICT

The truth about fear is that it's just a signal. It's a signal that is learned and reinforced.

Imagine that you were one of those crazies who decides to jump in the ocean, in a shark tank, surrounded by Great White sharks.

You are intentionally jumping into an environment laced with danger and many variables that you cannot control. But one thing is certain: the cage cannot be broken.

Well, ok, maybe the cage *could* be broken, but I have never heard of one being broken and, for the point of the illustration, *this* cage is constructed by God himself.

If the cage cannot be broken, then all the shark can do is rattle the cage. It can't get through the gaps between the bars and it can't unlock the door. All it can do is rattle the cage! But for many of us, we interpret the rattle as an indication that our fortress is breached. That our structure has been demolished and that's when poise turns to panic. We start flailing around with our arms outside of the cage, or worse yet, get out of the cage and start swimming for the boat! Bad idea!

I know that most of us wouldn't choose to jump in that cage. But if you are reading this book, then you are engaged in a journey that is even crazier, more challenging, and less predictable than diving with sharks. The journey of growing toward your greatest potential is the hardest thing we have ever taken on.

Just like the presence of those sharks, one of the most fundamental elements of that journey is the presence of fear. Fear, won't be completely eradicated or go extinct, but that doesn't mean that it has power. We can learn to engage with it differently.

Fear is not a verdict etched in stone. It's really just a suggestion based on what we've experienced.

When fear hits, we think we know what's going to happen based on what we have seen in the past. Maybe when you were playing your sport in high school or college the presence of fear caused you to tense up and throw up a shot that you would never take when playing with your friends. Maybe a client asked you to come out to work with their company on your kid's birthday and you panicked and complied. Or maybe when a situation got difficult during the game, you hid yourself and didn't say another word.

If that's what happened when fear hit in the past, we often expect the same outcome in the future and it causes us to operate in a certain manner.

I arrived early and was sitting outside JJ's school one day waiting to pick Amy and JJ up for lunch. Amy was in the basement hanging art for JJ's art show. Suddenly, a tornado siren went off across Denver. It was a beautiful day and I quickly realized that the siren was a test.

But the siren did something different to Amy. She started texting me asking me to come into the basement to take cover. Clearly, it made her panic for a bit. A few minutes later she texted and assured me that I didn't have to worry because it was just a test. I just shook my head and laughed.

What Amy and I did with the signal was completely different. See, the signal can't do anything to you. But how you learn to interpret the signal will dictate what actions you consistently take. Fear has no direct impact on a situation. What impacts our situation is how we interpret and *use* fear.

Notice I said *use* it. Don't ignore it. Sweeping things under the rug is a horrible strategy. Acting like the fear is not there only causes us to focus on it more. We need to embrace it as a signal. But for many of us, that signal of fear leads us to a place of panic and anxiety. But we can retrain that signal to mean, "This is where the goodness happens!"

Retrain The Signal

I walked into the empty banquet hall and saw hundreds of tables covered in white dishes and silverware. As I made my way toward the stage to set my things down, I noticed that every place setting had the same agenda facing up. Front and center was a picture of my face.

That's when I felt the eerie feeling in my gut that whispered, "Oh, Shit!" Again, I'm not cursing to be cultural. That's exactly what I heard.

As the banquet hall filled with a thousand people, I started to feel tense. When the various coaches and administrators came up on stage to talk about their teams, the fear increased.

I looked at the agenda and the last bullet read: Main Speaker – Jamie Gilbert. The rest of the page was blank! That's it, Jamie, you are the last act!

I felt my heart begin to race. It was one of those moments where it feels like your pulse is bulging out of your neck and everyone can see it. My mind tipped toward thoughts of inadequacy and moments where I did not give my best presentations in the past. That's what fear does. Like the smell of fresh-cut grass, it brings to mind vivid memories and feelings from the past. But fear usually elicits memories of your worst blunders.

I knew in that moment that fear was present. I also knew that it had *no* power. It could not determine anything. It was just a signal. Where I used to interpret that signal as "Jamie, you are going to screw up," the signal became, "This is where the goodness happens!"

I looked at my notes, and thought of the very first line I was going to say. I thought about how I wanted to walk to the stage. I visualized pausing when I got to the podium, and imagined the ideal pitch and pace of my voice as I uttered my first words.

I ran through this maybe four or five times while taking slow breaths for the next 15 minutes, until it was my time to speak.

I felt like it was one of the best talks I had given in a long time. Whether it was or wasn't doesn't matter. What matters is that I didn't buy into the signal that would have elicited a very terrible talk. I had learned to lean into the fear and embrace it as a necessary part of the journey. The more I embrace that signal in life, I find my anxiety turns to excitement. It moves me from paralysis to action, and moves me from thoughts of inadequacy to thoughts of execution.

EXPERIENCING THE FEAR MAY BE EXACTLY WHAT YOU NEED

During World War II, Germany used fear as one of it's greatest weapons. It wasn't the fear of experience, it was really the fear of expectation that paralyzed its enemies.

For a great period of time, people across Britain were paralyzed by the fear that came from bombing sirens. When the sirens would blare, entire cities would shut down for days, taking shelter from what they expected. It crippled the economy and caused extreme panic.

But when the bombs actually started to fall, things changed. The exposure to the reality of the bombings created less anxiety. The experience of the bombing raids actually caused Brits to get to work and fight. Eventually, the sirens would go off without causing anyone to stop what they were doing. They just kept working on creating the weapons and materials needed to win the fight.

It was experiencing what they feared most that really set them free. Sometimes, we need to experience what terrifies us because as we do, we often realize that it's really not that bad.

A Few Good Seconds

Often times, all we need is a few good seconds of courage to create clarity and take back control. I remember reading a study that discussed how taking a deep breath and pausing for three seconds actually allows us to see a situation with greater objectivity and clarity. It provides us with the opportunity to acknowledge the situation and respond instead of react.

Reactions are usually very quick, extremely emotional, and rarely see the whole picture.

A response, in my book, is methodical and tempered. It observes the situation instead of obsessing over it. A response does what is most constructive and keeps on moving.

It's the *keep on moving* part that is most essential.

The more you choose to embrace the fear and lean in in various capacities in your life, the more you will *use* fear in your sport, your business, and leadership.

It may be three seconds, it may be nine seconds, or it may be longer, but leaning into fear will help you experience that what you were afraid of was really not worth fretting over at all. The consistency of your willingness to lean in and "ask for the fork," really lays the foundation of you living out your own personal greatness.

- What are the signals that trigger fear in your life?
- How do you typically react when those sirens go off?
- How would you like to respond in those situations?
- What are two fears that you can deliberately lean into over the next ten days?

- P R I N C I P L E   2 2 -

Absorb The Anxiety

———

I'LL NEVER FORGET THIS DAY in Ireland. It was at the height of the economic crisis in Europe and it was right in the middle of our semester at the Irish Bible Institute.

Ireland had gone from one of the fastest growing economies in the world, to one of the worst economies in Europe, all in about two years. There were companies going bankrupt left, right and center. Banks were even being nationalized. Everywhere you looked in the papers and on television was doom and gloom.

I remember we were eating lunch in the café at the college when our founder and headmaster walked in and asked for our attention. There was an article in the paper that day detailing that the charitable giving sector was to be the hardest hit by the collapsing economy. We were a small college that was largely run on donations. Needless to say, our future looked very bleak.

Jacob called our attention while holding his cup of coffee and gave one of the most profound talks I have ever heard.

He told us that though things looked bleak in the economy, he was sure about one thing: Who God is.

He had seen God provide in *his* life and reminded us to remember God's hand in *our* lives. He told us not to dwell on the future of IBI, for no one could control that, but to remain faithful to our studies and seeking God's will in our lives. He said it was *his* job to speak with people about funding, and it was *God's* role to be the provider.

It was not so much *what* he said that impacted me, but *how* he made me feel. It was as if, in that moment, someone had awakened me from a bad dream and I realized things weren't so scary.

He didn't promise grandiose things that he couldn't deliver. He didn't promise that everything would be ok. He didn't dwell on how we should not worry. But with conviction in who God is, he absorbed every ounce of anxiety that was in my soul.

Essentially he got me away from thinking about uncontrollables (the future of IBI), pointed me back to a fundamental truth (who God is), and redirected me toward controllable action (take care of your studies).

His talk couldn't have been more than a minute, but the way he carried himself made me feel like it was a foregone conclusion that the funding would arrive, or at least something awesome would happen. It did. They received more money in donations than they had ever received before.

BACK TO CONTROLLABLES

I'm sure you've played on a team with someone who was an absolute game-changer. When she was at the game, you felt like you and your team couldn't be stopped. But when she wasn't there, or at least not in the game, suddenly things became very shaky.

It's interesting how your teammate's presence can radically affect you and everyone around you. It's not really that your teammate's presence means you are going to win the game. It's that her presence, and her focused demeanor, allow you to forget about the results and operate with freedom in what you can control.

The number one thing people tell me that plagues their performance and saps their energy is worrying about results. However, when the results are no longer our point of focus, and operating in controllables is, the results usually trend upward. That's exactly what absorbing the anxiety does.

Joshua asks a great question when we gather for our workshops, and it's one you need to grapple with: What do people consistently get when they get *you*?

Are you someone who is constantly in organizations of chaos? Are you someone who is consistently dealing with or surrounded by drama? If so, it's likely you are fueling that fire.

Our anxiety not only fuels the anxiety in others, but it can also create anxiety where none was previously present.

Fuel The Recovery Not The Anxiety

Amy and I learned rule number one very quickly when working with kids in Ireland: when a kid falls down or gets hit in the face with a ball, do not run over to help that kid.

I know it sounds ridiculously backward and goes against every natural impulse, but rushing over to the kid usually causes him to panic and think that his face has been completely split open. As you stop the game and draw everyone's attention to the boy on the ground, he starts to feel embarrassed or feel like there is blood gushing everywhere, which is usually what brings on the tears and a flood of uncontrollable emotion.

I can't tell you how many times I actually created anxiety when there was none, but if you stay calm, give a thumbs up, or even smile - do something that acknowledges that he is seen by you - the boy usually jumps back up and continues playing. We need to learn to fuel the recovery, not the anxiety.

Our experience matches these words of wisdom from the great philosopher Shaquille O'Neal: "When the General is calm, the troops are calm, too."

Calm doesn't mean you are in a constant state of relaxation. It doesn't mean that you are reclining in a beach chair without a care in the world. It's that you have developed the ability to stay focused on principles when everything around you and your team is crumbling. It doesn't mean that you don't see the circumstances around you, but that your circumstances don't dictate how you have to act.

Do those you lead trust you? I don't mean it like they trust that you could keep a secret. I mean, do they trust that you are highly trained and have the ability to thoughtfully and effectively navigate them through the chaos on the playing field and in their lives?

Who is someone you know who has your trust? Who is someone you are around or have been around who eases *your* anxiety in life? They don't do it through magic and it's not something they were born with.

When I study and meet with people who consistently absorb anxiety, that characteristic comes through experience and practice. If you are not placing yourself in situations where you have to experience difficult circumstances regularly, you cannot practice the ability to absorb anxiety.

It's one thing to talk about the Path to Mastery; it's another to *be* on the Path to Mastery.

It's one thing to speak about talking to yourself instead of listening to yourself; it's another to consistently practice that when your heart rate is over 160 bpm's.

It's one thing to talk about being willing to fail; it's another to put your job on the line in order to live up to your values and mission.

When you are engaging in circumstances that you know are going to be taxing, you are actively training the ability to absorb the anxiety in others around you.

- Who has absorbed your anxiety in situations in the past?
- What did they specifically do or not do that helped you?
- What are some contexts where you have created anxiety where none existed in the first place?
- What are you involved in now that stretches you and is refining that ability to exude poise instead of panic in really difficult circumstances?

Who You Become And The Effect You Have On Others

————

THIS WAS NOT SUPPOSED TO be how it turned out. I studied at one of the top universities in America, I was training with a top professional soccer team, and I had plenty of job opportunities in the States. But there I was, in Dublin, Ireland at an outdoor fruit market in the pouring rain, hustling cucumbers and kiwis.

I was sitting in the rain with a leaky umbrella that was held down by sacks of potatoes when I realized I had dug myself a hole. I was stewing over an interaction with my boss and a few of my colleagues that had left me boiling with anger. Because of my attitude, I had on blinders, only being able to find reasons why I felt they sucked at what they did and sadly, why they sucked at life!

That's terrible, I know. But that is where my mind was at the time. I was angry and bitter.

I decided a few weeks earlier that I was going to look for a new job because I had issues with how this one was run ethically, how people were treated, and that it was a hazardous environment.

One day, after my boss blew up on me, I felt like quitting right then and there, telling him where to shove his fruit and his apron! Though that's how I felt in the moment, I knew I was going to work there a little longer, so I realized I had a choice: I could make my time there about the job, or I could focus on who I was becoming.

Chances are you've been there, too. It seems like every week I get the same phone call from an assistant coach who is fed up with how his head coach leads.

"He brings someone in to talk to the players about trust, but no one on the team can trust *him*."

"She always points out the mistakes the players make and *never* talks about the things they do well."

I get the same call from players.

"The guys on my team are *always* treating me terribly and won't get me the ball."

"The coach isn't giving me quality minutes in the game to show what I can do."

Now, I am not saying that those statements aren't true. I'm quite certain the situations are stressful and difficult. But, it's never really about the situation. You see, we always have a choice in our perspective and attitude. It's not the situation that really hurts us, it's the meaning we give that situation that can eat us alive. If Dr. Ben Carson is right in saying "The person, flesh and blood, who has the most say over you in this world is you," then we have a choice.

Though I didn't *feel* like it, I chose to use the rest of my time there to learn about business, people, and communication. Instead of cringing when the man in the fedora would show up (who always haggled every last cent), I met the challenge with a smile and tried to get to know him better.

Instead of complaining about my boss not sending me a working measuring scale to price the fruit (the *one* essential in selling produce), I did the best I could with what I had and pre-packaged as much as possible and priced the bags, individually.

Instead of stewing the night before about my supervisor not giving correct signs for the pricing, I spent $10 on post-its and markers and made colorful signs myself.

But one day stands out above the rest. There was an elderly lady who came every week and complained about our produce. On this day, all my friends at the market saw her walking up and began talking trash about her. So I saw the opportunity.

"Good morning ma'am! How's your morning been?" I asked enthusiastically.

"Me Jeasus! Look at the weather. You know very well how my morning has been!" she replied. For what it's worth, if you live in Ireland, you *choose* to be there and you *know* it is going to rain three hundred days out of the year. Get on with it!

A few minutes later I asked if there was anything I could help with, and she retorted, "I can't believe your pineapples aren't Irish!"

I took a deep breath before I responded. In my head I thought *"Of course they aren't from Ireland you dumb _____! They need sun to grow!"*

So I smiled and said, "I understand your frustration ma'am. It's hard to get pineapples from Ireland because we're rarely blessed with sunshine." Talking about the weather and blaming it for how miserable we are is a sure-fire way to get an Irish person on your side!

I continued, "I love a pinneapple upside down cake as much as the next person! But if you're going to have that tonight for dessert, something will have to do. Our's are organic and I'd love to slice one up and give you a taste to try."

She agreed, took a bite and bought two pineapples. My interaction with her never really changed things between us. We can never change people. They have to choose to change. But I did what I could consistently do to make the environment as optimal as possible.

People always ask me where I learned to speak publicly and I usually come back to the fruit markets. Every day was an opportunity to refine my communication skills, and I had no earthly idea that the choices I made at the markets were training skills in me to speak, write, and lead in various capacities with Train To Be Clutch.

The funny thing about focusing on who you are becoming, is that it radically transforms the situation you are in. Suddenly, there is purpose in the struggle, and usually it elicits our deepest levels of creativity and highest levels of execution.

The Effect You Have On Others

I was walking around Belmont University's campus a few years back while talking with one of the guys I get to work with. He was getting ready to play in a professional golf tournament and we were going over things in his preparation.

I had told him many times that the only things that *really* matter are who he becomes and the effect he has on others in the process. But I decided to change tact.

With my friend on the phone and my headphones on, I walked up to a stranger who was walking to his next class. I called him over and said, "Excuse me sir, can I ask you a question? Do you know what PGA event is being played this week, where it's at, and who is expected to win?"

He gave me one of those puzzled looks you see when Conan O'Brien has someone interview people on the street, asking them who the current Vice President is.

Confused, he said, "Ummmmmm.....dude I'm sorry. I have absolutely no idea."

I replied, "No worries, man. Have a great day!"

My friend started cracking up on the other end of the phone because he got it. Even though he plays at the highest level in the world, how he plays golf will have very little effect on largely five billion people around the world.

He ended up having a great tournament posting a score of -18, coming in second place on the very last putt of the tournament.

When we got on the phone the next week I asked him about the week. He said the tournament really wasn't about golf at all. There was a young boy who he talked with the day before the tournament whom he connected with. He gave the family tickets to the tournament and he spent the rest of the weekend just trying to pour into that boy. His literal response to me was, "Jamie, it wasn't even about golf. I just tried to love on that one kid."

It's interesting that when we focus less on doing well in our task, and focus more on providing value, our performance of the task is not only better executed, but more enjoyable and meaningful.

As Daniel Pink has found through research, "The most deeply motivated people - not to mention the most productive and satisfied - hitch their desires to a cause larger than themselves."[19]

Maybe my mom was right after all! She used to always say that things are usually less about me and more about other people. I hated hearing that when I was growing up because I wanted it to be about me! If I'm honest, that still doesn't make situations any easier.

But it's amazing how our best work, and most creative solutions come when we are focused on providing for, engaging with, or empowering others. Regardless of where you are and what you are doing, the most important things are who you become and the effect you have on others.

- What are some key characteristics you can be working on developing right now in your context?
- If you look outside of your role or job, what kind of larger impact can you have, or are you having, on people outside of yourself and team?

All Your Work Won't Be Done Today

———

"So did you go straight from college golf to the PGA Tour?" I asked. I was visiting and working with a gentleman who has been on the Tour for the better part of a decade.

He laughed and said, "No," in a way that told me there was a good story.

He said he actually came out and worked at the same course in Arizona that he plays out of now. At the time, he was cleaning golf balls, washing clubs, and parking cars. In his downtime he was practicing golf and traveling all over the country, playing mini-tour events on his own dime. Later that year he went to Qualifying School (Q-School) to play in a tournament in order to qualify for the PGA Tour. He didn't make it.

So, he came back to his home course. For the next year, he scrubbed the same golf balls, washed the same clubs, and parked the same cars. He practiced in his downtime and traveled all over the country playing mini-tour events. He went to Q-School again and didn't make it.

So he came back to the same course and went through the same process - scrubbing the same golf balls, washing the same clubs, and parking the same cars. He practiced in his downtime and traveled all over the country playing mini-tour events. He went to Q-School and missed it, again, this time by just one stroke.

He went back to the course and scrubbed the same balls, washed the same clubs, and parked the same cars. He practiced in his downtime and traveled all over the country, went to Q-School and didn't make it.

Back to Arizona. Same balls, same clubs, same cars, same training routine, and went to Q-School. This time, he made it on the number.

Five years of growth and delayed gratification!

What I know is that most of us will not put in that kind of work for something we say that we truly want. But his story wasn't as powerful as his answer to my next question:

"If you didn't make it on that fifth year, would you have given up?"

"No," he said, "I always felt like I was getting better and truly believed it was just a matter of time before I could play at that level."

Every week I talk with people who are going to pursue playing professional sports. The most common thing people tell me is that they are going to give it a season, a year, or two years. My immediate thought is, *"You are creating your greatest impediment."*

ALL YOUR WORK WON'T BE DONE TODAY

One of the greatest inhibitors to your personal and collective greatness is trying to accelerate the process.

We have already talked about how, if we are honest, we want grandiose gains every day and in every area of our life. But that's not how it works. Buildings get built brick-by-brick. Websites are fashioned code-by-code. Jump shots are refined rep-by-rep. Parenting is done moment-by-moment, day-by-day.

There are way too many people in sports who are practicing to feel better rather than get better. They are trying to work on every area of their game at every practice. Or worse yet, they are only working on their deficiencies every practice. All this, with a view to excel in the next tournament, next game, or even the next practice. Simply put: little worthwhile work gets done.

I have a friend and client who is pursuing basketball as a professional career. Right now he has a crazy amount of anxiety in school, relationships with his coaches and parents, and he is treating himself quite poorly. On top of that, his practice is rushed, filled with tension, and sporadic in terms of what skills are being honed. I asked him this question recently: *If you knew that you were going to be starting in the NBA in three years, what would change for you right now?*

It was like a pressure release valve was hit and you could literally hear the freedom in the way he spoke. Sounding like someone had removed their hands from his neck, he said, "I'd probably relax a lot more. I wouldn't be rushing everything every day when I play. I know that I would focus on learning things better rather than just trying to look good. I'd probably enjoy things in basketball a lot more."

"What about outside of basketball?" I asked.

"Yeah, I know I'd be kinder to my parents. I'd actually be present with my friends and not be stressing about basketball all of the time."

This question shows us two things. It elicits the fact that how they train, treat themselves, interact with others, and basically live life is in accordance with the likelihood of a result. In his case, playing in the NBA.

But it also shows that what gets in the way of us truly learning and genuinely interacting is the timeline we suspect things must follow. If we have a definite timeline in mind, things seem to be more manageable. But there is little in life that has a definite timeline. Especially when it comes to developing people.

Not only do we need to surrender the result, we need to surrender our timeline.

Equipping Takes As Long As It Takes
You cannot cram forty years of life experience into a six-week course on character. Nor can you expect that everyone in college will accept forty years of wisdom in their four years of college. You don't get a top-level consultant onboard and then start playing the best you ever have. I know that isn't the best pitch for my

workshops, but it's the truth. Teaching can happen in an hour, but equipping takes as long as it takes.

So my question to people coaching is, "Do you want to *equip* people or simply *change* people?" I know what we would *say* we want, but what we *truly* want is evidenced by our actions.

I had a person who coaches at the Division 1 level tell me that the whole team came to practice the other day lacking energy and focus. They have instituted many of our tools to help their team adjust, but the coach asked, "Jamie, what do you do in THAT situation?"

"Let me ask you this," I said. "How many games in past seasons has this same lack in focus occurred?"

"More than a few games," she admitted.

"So, if it's very likely that the majority of our team will have a night like this during *this* season, then we need to help equip them to adjust."

First, we need to have a shift in perspective. If you notice that the majority of the team is struggling in this way, let's decide, as a staff, that a *successful practice* will now be one in which we help the players adjust their focus. Nevermind points, efficiency of inbound plays, tactics, or whatever else you had written out on your practice plan. Today's main focus is helping them adjust their mental state. It's becoming an opportunity to help them figure out how to harness their emotions and collectively move toward doing what's most constructive.

How often is *that* on the practice plan?

Here is the thing: yelling at them, threatening them, and even punishing them with running or some other form of fitness is not equipping. It's creating an aversion. It's creating fear. Yes, getting them on the line will certainly get the energy up in *that* practice, but it does not equip them to learn how to adjust. Getting that immediate change feels good, because it makes practice look better, but really all we are doing is creating a culture of fear and people who are co-dependent on an authority figure to kick them into gear.

Usually when I see a coach get upset about one of *those* practices, I want to ask my wife's favorite question: *"Who's the toddler in this situation?"* In other words, you, as the adult, flipping out because of a circumstance around you, are modeling the *very thing* we are asking our players not to do.

The mark of an adult, and someone who is becoming transformational in their coaching, is the ability to deviate from your practice plan, to throw out your perceived timeline, and instead address an issue and challenge that is much deeper and integral to your season and the lives of the people you get to lead.

It's simple: equipping has no definitive timeline. However, we can certainly delay the process of growth by trying to make people "get it" right now.

I love this question and I challenge you to stop and answer it honestly: *If you knew that you were going to get whatever result you want in three years, what would that change for you right now?*

How would you treat people?

How would you look at mistakes?

How would you look at your time?

Further, let's make sure we follow that up with even better questions: *If you knew you would have the opportunity of your dreams in thirty days, three months, or three years, how would you spend your time right now?*

What commitments would you invest in?

Who do you want to become in the process?

What effect do you want to have on others?

Too many of us are like the kid at the arcade, wanting the massive teddy bear that costs one thousand tickets, when really our level of investment has left us with seven tickets. All we can afford is a spider ring or an eraser from the glass case in front.

I don't care what you want. I care about what you are willing to surrender. I care about what you are willing to invest. And I care about how long you are willing to engage in the process of growth, because the greatest predictor of future success is the ability to delay gratification.

- Do you consider yourself as someone who can delay gratification?

- What kind of things fall into the equipping category that might not fall into the coaching category for you?
- In one of your last practices or work days, what would have changed if you had focused on long term equipping instead of short term compliance?

Free To Fail

———

YOUR UNWILLINGNESS TO FAIL IS killing us all. Your unwillingness to be vulnerable and really be seen, is not only holding you back, but it's crushing your organization and it's killing your family.

I went to watch one of my college basketball teams play recently, and the game really tore me up. Not because they lost, but because of *how* they lost. Our opponents had a player drop 35 points on us and 18 of those points came from three-point range. The painful part was that all of these points came from running the same exact play over and over.

They ran a simple screen at the top of the key that caused one of our guys, let's call him John, to make a decision. After the screen he had a choice: he could hedge and he could step out towards the guy who was shooting (who they knew was a great three-point shooter), or John could retreat and cover the bigger player, *his* player, who was turning and going down low for a simple dump and dunk.

Everyone in the gym could see it coming. John made the same decision over and over: go after the big player, *his* player, and protect the paint. He believed he was "doing his job." But really he was making the other team's job very *very* easy: knock down uncontested threes.

After the game I was chatting with the coaches and connecting again. I asked one of them if they prepared in the scout for this dude who shot the three, and I said that with a smile, certain that they had. The coach just smirked and shook his head, disappointingly saying "Yes."

"Our guy wasn't willing to be vulnerable."

"What do you mean?" I asked, intrigued.

"John would rather say 'I'm doing *my* job because *my* player didn't score' instead of hedging, putting pressure on the shooter and causing a harder shot. We told him even if the big player caught the ball he had such a bad percentage at scoring inside the paint that we would take the few points he scored."

John chose not to do it. Again and again he avoided vulnerability. He chose not to be exposed. He didn't want it on the stat sheet that his player scored X amount of points. He cared more about what it looked like, rather than what it actually was.

I've been there, and I know you have too. I wonder what you're holding on to? I wonder what you are choosing to hoard? I wonder what you are afraid to do because of your fear of being vulnerable?

It's not comfortable writing this book. It's not comfortable writing *any* book. It's not comfortable telling stories about myself and I know it's not comfortable when people tell me their own stories. But this book came out of a place of vulnerability. It came out of a place where someone told me, "Jamie, we need your story." I know these stories are opening me up to ridicule. Like a fighter lying prone and open on the canvas, vulnerability feels unsafe and, undoubtedly, uncomfortable.

John's team needed him to embrace the unsafe. They needed him to lean into what was uncomfortable. And we need *you* to do the same.

Your organization is struggling because you're not willing to be fully seen. Your team is flailing because you're not willing to take the shot. Your team is languishing because you're not willing to treat people like people because you have to "keep your job." Your family's growth is stunted because you attend to making things look good instead of using your time to steward what you know you need to steward.

Don't Call People Out. Call People Up.

I have a dear friend who I wholeheartedly admire. She does bold and courageous things every day. In her industry, especially in her position, you tell people what to do and then you "hold them accountable."

Accountability is one of my least favorite words. Every time I hear it I get the picture of a person in authority hiding out behind a bush with a hammer in hand waiting to catch those they lead getting it wrong so they can jump out, whack them on the head, and gratifyingly yell, "See? I knew you'd mess up!" It's interesting that that's the same image many have of God.

We need less accountability for others, and more vulnerability with ourselves. A friend of mine mentioned a segment by Anderson Cooper on the Pope, and recalled this line, "The Pope does not call people out. He calls them up." And what a beautiful picture of what Joshua calls *advocay* leadership.

Think about Jesus as our greatest advocate. He is totally for us, and loves us unconditionally, but he holds us to a high standard. And it's that union of high standards and deep *deep* love that allows us to move forward and grow.

But you cannot call people up if you are not in the midst of your own journey towards growth. You need to grapple in your own battle before you dip in the pit of others'. We don't need you to hold others accountable, we need you to be an advocate: deep deep love, high controllable standards.

My friend is an advocate. She has stepped out in faith. She's trusted me and has embraced the belief that people can make great decisions. They just need an environment that allows them to do that. So what does she do? She asks questions as much as she gives directives. And she actually lets her kids answer. She is working on reducing her words by almost 50%. She is trying to treat her kids like people.

She has surrendered the need to keep her job in order to live the mission of equipping young women for life through sport. She is laying down the weapons of shame and threat and instead creates a culture of love and autonomy. Guess what? Her kids are not the same.

My friend tells me she feels like she is failing more often than not, but we both know that real change cannot be forced. There is a crazy amount of change in her program, and I see it every time I visit.

If she wants her kids to be vulnerable, to live out their passions, and really give their absolute best, she needs to model it. And she does. More than words of encouragement and more than threats and directives, her kids need to see her being vulnerable.

I need your vulnerability. We need your willingness to fail, and just like my friend, you'll find that your failures are just the beginning of your greatness. They are the necessary repetitions that tear down muscle fibers so that they can fuse together stronger. When vulnerability becomes a lifestyle, you'll embrace a life of freedom and elicit freedom for those you get to influence.

Again, what are you holding on to or holding back? What is it that you are afraid of? Usually, I find for myself and others that it's either the fear of what others will think or the fear how things will work out in the future. I use this question as a barometer in my life: "Am I operating out of love or fear?"

Am I making a run on the field because I'm fearful that if I don't, my coach will pull me out?

Am I not writing a story because I'm afraid of how others will take it?

Am I staying in college because I'm afraid that I won't have a degree or anything to show if I just relentlessly pursued my passion?

Usually, we know the answer, and if you are being held back by the fear of what it looks like or the fear of how it will all turn out, you will choose a life of fearful living. You will elicit fear in those you get to influence and/or you will continue to "fit in" for the wrong reasons instead of standing out for the right reasons.

Operating out of love is choosing to do what you believe is right, most beneficial, and what you are passionate about. It's doing it regardless of what people think now or will think in the future. It's doing it without knowing what the exact return on investment will be.

Write the book because you deeply care for the *one* person it will speak to.

Stay in or go to college because *you* want to experience it and study a particular field.

Hit the golf ball the way *you* want to hit it and know you can.

Treat those you lead like *people* because you know that's what truly matters.

Operating out of love is a bold and courageous strategy and does not promise that you will get exactly what you want. But operating out of fear doesn't mean you'll get those results either. You have to choose your strategy. And your choice will create your challenge, and the challenge for others around you. But your choice will aslo create your chance, and the chance for everyone who's with you.

Walk The Talk

Living a life of love is living a life of vulnerability. That's exactly what Stephanie modeled. She was overcome with emotion as she told me about her situation. Her boss made it clear that her job was on the line. If the team didn't at least win their conference, she would be unemployed.

With tears flowing freely, she sobbed that she was not going to treat her girls like numbers. She was not going to step on their necks and she was not going to threaten or shame them. "If this is my last year here, the girls are going to know how much I love them."

Stephanie has a family. Stephanie has a house. She is part of a community that has deep roots. One would say that she has a lot to lose. But in surrendering the results she gained so much more.

She stuck to her convictions and loved her girls regardless of their performance.

Stephanie's team didn't win conference, but they played beautifully all year long and probably had better results than they were capable of. Regardless of how she felt, she lived a life of love.

Stephanie, your courage to not only share that story and emotion, but to embrace your principles, regardless of circumstances, challenges me every day.

A life of vulnerability is a life of courage.

A life of vulnerability is a life of truth.

A life of vulnerability is a life of growth.

A life of vulnerability is a life fully lived.

Your life of vulnerability might just save countless lives across the world.

No one has yet seen what you are able to provide and produce when you begin standing out for the right reasons, instead of fitting in for the wrong reasons.

- If you had to place a percentage on how many decisions you make out of fear vs. love, what would that percentage be?
- When have you made decisions out of fear in the past?
- When have you made decisions to operate out of love in the past?
- What decisions are you grappling with right now? What would it look like if you made that decision according to what you think is right, most beneficial, or what you feel most passionate about? Acknowledge the fear. Operate out of love.

We Are Going To The Other Side

———

THERE IS A TRUE STORY about a group of fishermen who were told to get in a boat that was going over to the other side of the lake. These men were skilled in their craft and had lived on the water. But as they got into the boat and started sailing, a huge storm kicked up with wind and rain so fierce they couldn't see five feet in front of them.

As the winds howled, the waves grew bigger and more furious, and the boat began to rock in a way they had never experienced before. With little sight and a shaky foundation beneath them, the cracks of thunder and bolts of lightning only added to their feelings of helplessness.

So, one of the men on the boat ran downstairs. You see, the guy who told them to get in the boat was a man named Jesus. He was a man of authority. Actually, He was the Son of God.

When one of the men came downstairs, Jesus was there snoozing with his head on a pillow.

The man flipped out on him yelling, "Jesus!!! Don't you care that we're about to die?!?"

Jesus opened an eye and gazed right into the eyes of that man, absorbing his anxiety and fear. So Jesus rose from his bed, climbed up to the deck of the boat and just told the storm to stop. The crazy thing is that it did. Like a tornado that decides its damage is done, the storm lifted and completely dissipated.

Jesus once again turned to the men and said, "Why are you afraid? You have so little faith!"

Now, I'll be honest, for a long time I thought Jesus was way too hard on the poor fellas. I mean I've been through plenty of tornadoes in Tulsa and *everyone* has *every* right to be scared!

I'm not sure if Jesus was laughing or if he was very stern, but I know Jesus didn't call them out. He called them up. He saw them right where they were, and they saw him right where he was, in the boat with them. His question and statement were not full of shame. They were full of honest love.

Interestingly, when you go back to the beginning of the story, what did Jesus say to them? He said, "Let us go to the other side of the lake."

Here He is, Jesus, a man of authority and the One who these guys believed was the Son of God, basically telling them that they *are* going to the other side, like it was a foregone conclusion.

Imagine meeting Steph Curry outside of Oracle Arena. He says, "Come on man, let's go inside and shoot around." Who he is, what he's done, and the authority he has in his position are all indicators that we shouldn't shudder or question whether or not it's actually going to happen. If you forget who you're with though, you turn around when you see the man in the yellow shirt that reads, "Security."

"C'mon, Steph! Let's get out of here!" you say, frightened. Steph just looks at you like you're crazy and says, "It's cool man, you're with *me*."

That's where the fishermen were. They forgot who Jesus was. They let their fear of the circumstance trump the truth of their God: God does not change. He can't.

Every time I read that story, I'm challenged *and* encouraged. Challenged because if I really believe that God is who He says He is, then I should not be living in fear. Notice I didn't say that fear won't come to me. It will, I just won't accept it.

The story encourages me because the disciples are just like me. God used them in a mighty way. They weren't super-qualified in speaking or well-versed in the Christian faith. They weren't people who had big followings or really brought much to the table in terms of abilities. Still, God used them to change the entire landscape of the world in which we live. Simply put, they weren't qualified, but they were *called*.

I don't know your story. I don't know your experiences. I don't know your particular situation, and I don't know your thoughts on Jesus. But I am fully convinced of this:

You are not your past.
You are not your performance.
You are not your potential.
You are perfectly and meticulously created for a purpose.
And God is waiting with open arms for you to embrace
him, and consistently lean on him fully.

The storms have come in your life, and I know they will continue
to come. We all have a choice when they arrive. *What* we choose
to hold on to as truth, and *how* we choose to act will determine
the lives we live.

We all have the power to choose. Choose wisely.

Jump And Keep Jumping

———

His son was so excited to hear about the trip! He couldn't believe his dad was taking him to Africa for a few weeks. Immediately, the kid started researching all the wildlife they were going to see while on their safari excursions.

One of the animals that soon stood out to him was the African Impala. The young boy had read that the Impala could leap up to ten feet high in a single bound. The kid was mesmerized as he thought of an Impala jumping right on top of the roof of his house.

A few weeks before the trip, the boy and his dad went to the city zoo to see some of the animals in the flesh. He couldn't wait to see the Impala. But when they got to the exhibit, they were stunned.

If you were a zookeeper and knew that the Impala could jump ten feet high, how tall do you think you would make the wall of their enclosure? Some of us who are trying to count the pennies might make it ten feet, but most of us would cover our bases and tack on an extra few feet just in case you had one of those LeBron James-like Impalas in your group.

Incredibly, the wall of the enclosure was only six feet high.

Perplexed, the kid's dad called a zoologist over and asked what was going on.

"I know it sounds crazy, but everything is safe," the zoologist said. "Even though the Impala can jump that wall easily, it won't. Only because of fear. If they cannot see that where they are going to land is safe, Impalas will not jump. They won't give up the security of their enclosure for the opportunity of freedom."

You Are Holding You Back

We, my friends, are in a society of Impalas - terrified to jump because we don't know what the return on our investment will be.

We don't know how it will all pan out. But we overestimate the comfort of a "sure thing." I've met many people who were invested in the sure thing. They had a well paying job that they tolerated. They were at a top-level academic institution only to have their scholarship cut. They received a degree from the most prestigious university in the country and still don't work in their desired field. They have married into a wealthy family and have the security of a comfortable lifestyle, but there is no love in the marriage. And some are in awesome missions, but the mission they really are passionate about has changed, and they know it.

I don't judge any of these people. I was once an Impala trapped in the zoo. I found myself dreaming from time to time of the security of returning to what is comfortable and a *sure bet*. And I often think about settling where I am now too.

It's not easy to jump. Especially when our families, friends, and coaches tell us we have no chance. But you don't have to have it all figured out to move forward.

LETTING GO OF SECURITY

Alan served as a coach for a girls high school basketball team for a decade, but he was stirred that it was time to move on. He shared his story in one of our workshops and openly admitted that his reservation in making a move was financial security.

In front of the whole group, Joshua asked him a simple question: "Alan, do you believe that Jesus is still on the throne?"

"Yes I do." He said with a certain nod.

"Then act like it." Joshua retorted.

I remember the tension not only in the room, but the tension in the concept. It's one thing to say that you believe something to be true. It's another to live according to that truth. It's not easy. It's very uncomfortable, and I felt just as convicted as Alan did.

Over the next few weeks, Alan prayed and spoke with his wife consistently on the matter. He called a few weeks later and had made the leap. He quit his job and was open for a move anywhere in the country. The opportunities started pouring in. His new job is not free from challenges and it has not given him ultimate freedom in time and finances. But in making that choice, he and his wife are better equipped to handle whatever will be thrown at them as they jump, when they know jumping is needed.

I wonder what security it is that you are unwilling to let go of at the cost of the opportunity on the other side? I'm not just talking about a job move, relocating, or any kind of business venture. I'm talking about who you are becoming. I'm talking about stepping out and just asking the people next to you a simple question. I'm talking about being willing to sow beneficial beliefs in your life, regardless how goofy it feels. I'm talking about choosing to equip your team through questions instead of instructing them through statements.

Applying these principles takes insane amounts of courage. And here's the secret: When you jump once, you must keep jumping again and again. All of these principles show up in my Principle Circle almost daily. I've never conquered any of them because they are not mountains to be summitted. They are timeless pieces of wisdom that serve as the tools for the climb.

Trust. Don't Lean.

———

A MENTOR OF MINE TOLD me a story about one of his clients who got to meet Mother Teresa. He was so excited and he asked her to pray for him.

She asked what she could pray specifically about. "Please pray that God would give me clarity around a few things and let me know which way to turn," he responded.

She said "No."

He couldn't believe it! He was thinking, "But you're *Mother Teresa*! You have to pray for me!"

She said, "I won't pray that God gives you clarity. God has promised wisdom, knowledge, and understanding to those who ask. But I will pray that God increases your faith to trust and move forward with what you know deep inside that you should do."

I think Mother Teresa was really speaking to me! I can't count how many times I have asked for clarity. How about you?

But what I've come to realize, is that God has already given us what we need to know. We don't need to know more. We usually need to do more with what we know. And as we do, we need to trust the one who holds us, and we need to trust the principles moving forward.

Honestly, I don't trust myself. I trust God and I trust intuition. I trust that living according to these principles will take me forward in greatness. That trust is an investment and it's a choice.

The writer of Hebrews put it this way: *Faith is the assurance of things hoped for, the conviction of things not yet seen.* It's an unwavering belief, even when the storms arise. It's a core commitment to trust in the Lord with all of your heart and not lean on your own understanding.[20]

It takes incredible courage to believe that God is the creator of the world. It also takes incredible courage not to believe that. It takes insane courage to fully commit to just about anything.

What I've found is that you do not jump once and find yourself free forever. Faith requires that we jump and keep jumping. For everyday we will be faced with walls and enclosures that we create or we allow society to create for us. Those structures aren't real. They are like the ant on a piece of paper. When you get him on the page and draw a circle around him with a sharpie, the ant won't leave the circle. So it is in our lives.

It takes incredible courage to jump. That jumping doesn't cease.

When Amy and I returned to the states in 2012, I had the insane notion that God wanted me to keep playing soccer. Amy was eight months pregnant. I had been out of soccer for almost two years. No teams knew about me and I had no way of reaching out to them. So I thought.

I was working for a friend in insurance answering phones when I decided I could reach out to a team. So I showed up to a pro team's practice, approached a coach, and asked if I could train with them.

He said yes! I entered the most taxing period of my life spiritually, physically, and emotionally. I never got a contract, but that team was a training ground for who I was becoming.

When I started training with the team a family member called me and wanted to talk. He laid into me about how irresponsible I was being, that it wasn't right that I was living with and off my father-in-law, that I wasn't providing for my family, and that I needed to get a *real* job and be responsible.

I was taken aback! It wasn't *his* life that was on the line. It wasn't *his* immediate family that was being affected.

So, I did it anyway. I jumped and kept jumping. I took the unsure bet. I immersed myself in training and in Train To Be Clutch. It wasn't out of spite, but out of love. It was out of a deep passion to follow the inklings of God's Spirit. I had no idea what would come of it, but I knew that the surest way to flail in life was to be irresponsibly responsible.

I realized something else. It *was* his life that was on the line. It *was* his immediate family that was being affected because every time you step out in faith for something you believe to be true, you challenge other people's paradigms. I didn't do that directly; it's just the byproduct of making choices.

We jumped and I thought everything would change between us as he saw the impact and influence through our work. But everything hasn't changed. He still thinks we are crazy, and that is fine. I still love him. I'm just around him a lot less.

When you jump, don't expect everyone to applaud you. Often the first jump only takes you to the beginning of the desert you must walk through towards greatness. And that desert can be a lonely place.

As you decide to make changes in how you operate and think, people will come at you. When you choose to stand out for the right reasons, instead of fitting in for the wrong reasons, there will be stones thrown and punches landed. But take comfort; this is resistance common to the journey.

THEY WILL COME AT YOU

I was at Whole Foods recently checking out while on the phone with my friend, Abby. I motioned to the lady at the checkout counter that I was on a call and I was sorry.

As she handed me the receipt she glared directly into my eyes, which stopped all of my movement.

Holding the other end of the receipt she said, "We are all being vulnerable, and we are all being seen. They will come at you, but do it anyways."

As I walked away, Abby asked what just happened and I told her that I was just prophesied over by a lady named Barbara.

"What did she mean when she said that?" Abby asked.

I knew straight away that though it could be people who might come at me for our next venture in life, that wasn't what she was getting at. She was talking about thoughts. And my how hard the next three months were.

I was in the midst of two book projects, a new live group mentoring program, two interns were living with us as a family, I was trianing close to 20 hours each week for soccer, I was traveling for work, our four month old Ava was not sleeping well, and it felt like nothing was getting accomplished.

During that time, onslaught after onslaught of limiting thoughts and destructive beliefs surfaced and wearied me. I'm always asked where our thoughts come from and I always respond that if Scripture is true, then Satan is the father of all lies and is heaving fiery darts at us all day long. Those thoughts aren't truth, but I have to choose whether to acknowledge them or accept them.

I don't tell this story to make you sad or make myself sound special. I share this story because it's been the reality of our pursuit in becoming who we feel called to be, and pursuing a dream destined to fail without divine intervention.

When you live according to principles and train yourself to adapt, pivot, and thrive, you do not eradicate resistance. You do not eliminate challenge. You are just better equipped for greater and greater moments.

I've been praying for you. There is no coincidence that you have picked up this book, and for that I am honored. But the wisdom in any book is only useful if applied. I know there is something inside of you that you know you want to act on but aren't pursuing.

My prayer for you is that God will illuminate the strongholds in your life, and walk with you in the journey of tearing them down. I pray that He will give you wisdom, knowledge, and understanding as you move forward in life. Most of all, I pray that you will have the courage to jump and keep jumping.

They will come at you. That's a fact.

The question is, are you going to hide in fear or move forward in trust?

The TRUTH Will Set You Free

THE PRINCIPLES IN THIS BOOK have been the truths that I have seen transform my life, and the lives of those around me. And no doubt, as you embrace them and grapple with applying them in your life, things will start to shift.

But there is also a singular TRUTH that is really the key to a completely new existence. It's the TRUTH that God created you, loves you, died for you, and is waiting for you to embrace Him fully and deeply. And as you do, there is a freedom that you can enter in that is unlike anything you've ever experienced.

Money won't fall from the skies. Hardships and resistance won't cease. But there will be a power in you and around you that will carry you along in the journey towards greatness.

This freedom is scary though. Because freedom often feels like irresponsibility. It feels irrespnsible not to dwell on mistakes and not to give in when resistance hits. It feels like we don't deserve it. It feels uncomfortable. It's like someone who leaves the military, finishes a prison sentence, or leaves a corporate job and starts their own business. They experience the scary side of freedom.

They dont have anyone telling them how to use their time. And they might not have anyone around them at all. And the most comfortable thing to do is return to confines and strictures of bondage. For many of us, that bondage is usually an anxious way of thinking and living.

The bondage might also be going back to what we've always done. To return to the familiar, and the seemingly secure. But security may be the stricture that is strangling your highest from of service to the world.

I'm not telling you to quit your job. But I'm not telling you to stay. I'm not telling you to drop out of school, break up with your boyfriend, sell the house, or start a for-purpose foundation. I'm asking you a question: If you knew, and fully believed that God is enough, that you are enough, and that there is enough around you to accomplish what is deeply burning in your heart, what would you do?

In my time conversing with people in various walks of life, I have found that *enough* is truly the issue. "Am I enough?" is the greatest fear in our society. And that stems from answering, "Is He enough?" The answer to that question will radically affect your veiw of yourself, others, and the possibilities and problems in this world.

He is Enough.

We are Enough.

There is Enough.

God once spoke these words to me, through a person I love. And I think they are words for you too. My prayer is not only that you hear them, but that you soak them in and dwell on them. That you do not resist them, but choose to act on them. That you see them as reality, and let go of perception. And the TRUTH will set you free.

I am the God of enough time,
Of enough wisdom,
Of enough patience,
Of enough in every situation.

Not of little,
Not of want,
Not of lack,
Not of sickness and hurt.

A servant to all who seek,
To all who look,
To all who call,
To all who hurt, deliverance.
A present help in time of need.

The Lord is victorious,
The Lord is right,
The Lord is there in wisdom and in truth.

Truth delivers,
Truth is the guide,
Truth is the bona fide,
Truth carries the weak and the wounded,

Truth makes light the wrong,
Truth defies explanation,
Truth is the Lord.

No stature,
No walk,
Or posture,
Can override Truth.

Truth delivers says the Lord.

Go!

THE STORMS ARE COMING AND the rules for the fight will always be in flux. Rarely will the circumstances in our lives meet our expectations if we only have one. But if you are one of the few who choose to collect principles and begin living according to those pieces of wisdom, the ropes will be back on the ring.

You may win some fights. You might lose some. You might even get knocked out a few times. But with the principles in place you can never fall out of the ring.

You are powerful beyond measure.

You are not alone.

You are not on trial.

You are free to fan your gifts into flame and tap into your own personal greatness.

For the sake of the generations to come, I pray that you do.

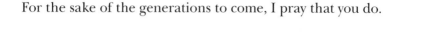

Thank you for taking the time to read my work! But wisdom only goes as far as it's applied. If you want the how-to guide on creating your circle, or if you want to see how others create their's, visit www.t2bc.com/pcircle.

And I would love to see your circle, so please share it with me!

Twitter: @Jdgilbert19
Instagram: @Jdgilbert19
Jamie@Traintobeclutch.com
#pcircle

T H A N K   Y O U ' S

Thank you Jesus for never folding your arms and truning away from me. Thank you for wisdom, knowledge, and understanding. And thank you for the journey to come.

Thank you Amy for you persistent love and constant joy in this journey together. Without you, the journey would be dull, there would be no book, and there would be no impact.

Thank you JJ for your patience and laughter! Your interjections in my writing to play Paw Patrol are some of the highlights of the journey.

Thank you Ava for smiling continuously!

Thank you Joshua for seeing potential in me when I couldn't see it myself. Thank you for not conforming to the patterns of this world and for continuing to be bold and courageous. Your loyalty and love are a constant encouragement to me and our family.

Thank you Mom and Dad for always encouraging us to chase our dreams. Your excitement in, and commitment to, creating opportunity for us is a model for how we want to parent our kids too! Thank you for your love for God, and your model of expectant and deep prayer.

Thank you Dad for absorbing my anxiety when Vanderbilt dropped the program. You have no idea what that meant to and for me.

Thank you Mom for interceding for me and countrless others. Your resolve to trust and share what God speaks to you challenges me deeply.

Thank you Tony for holding me to a high standard and loving me deeply. You were right, more might be done for the kingdom of God over coffee and bowls of soup than all the programs and outreaches across the world.

Thank you Jacob for teaching me what it means to trust in the Lord and not lean on our own understanding.

Thank you Jim and Katie for your constant love and support over the years. Without you we could not have made this dream a reality.

Thank you Cameron for being such a great friend and for never settling. Your commitment to people and your own personal growth challenges me daily.

Thank you Cara for trusting me and doing the dirty hard work that many others are unwilling to do. I mean what I said, I think you could radically alter the way the world looks at coaching.

Thank you Gerrod for your love, your depth of care, and your timely words. I'm blown away by your belief in people and your trust in the Lord.

Thank you Greg for your whimsy, fearlessness in saying what needs to be said, and your commitment to Joshua and I. The story you have lived and continue to live makes me want to take on the world!

Thank you Father, for your steadfast love. I know that you don't change, and that I am never alone.

WORKS CITED:

1. James Altucher, *Choose Yourself: Guide To Wealth*

2. John G. Miller, *The Question Behind The Question*

3. Carol Dweck, *The New Psychology Of Success*

4. *Eternal leadership Podcast,* John Ramstead and Steve Reiter, www.eternalleadership.com/024/

5. James Clear, *This Coach Improved Every Tiny Thing By One Percent And Here's What Happened,* http://jamesclear.com/marginal-gains

6. Mark Batterson, *In A Pit With A Lion On A Snowy Day*

7. Austin Kleon, *Steal Like An Artist*

8. Marianne Williamson, *A Return To Love: Reflections on the Principles of "A Course in Miracles"*

9. James Clear, *How To Stick With Good Habits Everyday By Using The Paper Clip Strategy,* http://jamesclear.com/paper-clips

10. Mark Batterson, *In A Pit With A Lion On A Snowy Day*

11. Bob Goff, *Love Does: Develop A Secretly Incredible Life In An Ordinary World.*

12. Ken Hoffman, *Every Person Has Infinite Worth*, TEDxSpokane
    https://youtu.be/E9fHCrP8hZM

13. Eugene Cho, *Overrated: Are We More In Love With The Idea Of
    Changing The World Than Actually Changing The World?*

14. Peter Bregman, *Four Seconds: All The Time You Need To Stop
    Counter-Productive Habits And Get The Results You Want*

15. John Gordon, *The Best Advice I've Ever Heard*, http://www.
    jongordon.com/blog/the-best-advice-ive-ever-heard/

16. 1 Corinthians 4:11-13

17. Carol Dweck, *Mindset: The New Psychology Of Success*

18. Greg McKeown, *The Disciplined Pursuit Of Less*

19. Daniel Pink, *Drive: The Surprising Truth About Motivation*

20. Proverbs 3:5